THE WILLS LAWYERS: THEIR STORIES OF:
Money, inheritance, greed, family and...
BETRAYAL

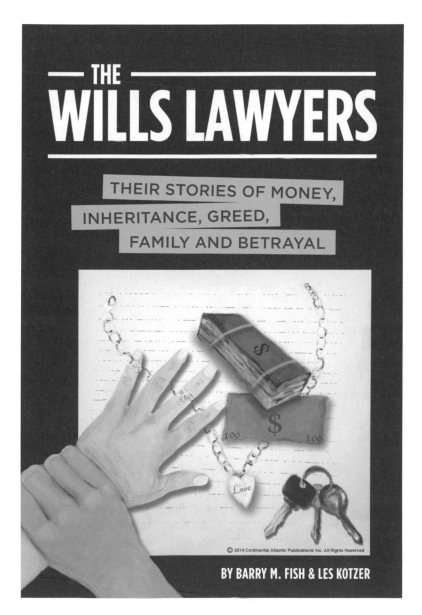

THE WILLS LAWYERS: THEIR STORIES OF:
Money, inheritance, greed, family and... BETRAYAL

ISBN: 978-0-9920847-2-1

All inquiries can be made to the following address:
c/o Continental Atlantic Publications, Inc.
7951 Yonge Street
Thornhill, Ontario, Canada
L3T 2C4
Telephone toll-free (U.S. and Canada) 1(877) 439-3999

Websites: www.familyfight.com
www.thefamilywar.com
www.aninheritance.com
www.willappointment.com
www.thewillslawyers.com

YouTube: The Wills Network
Email: leskotzer@familyfight.com
bfish@fishlaw.ca

The discussions in this book should not be considered as legal or financial advice. It is strongly suggested that if you do require such advice, you should consult a professional advisor in your jurisdiction. Accordingly, if you wish to take any steps as a result of reading this book, please consult such advisor before doing so. The laws governing the various topics discussed in this book will vary depending upon the jurisdiction.

Printed and Bound in Canada

ABOUT THE AUTHORS

Barry M. Fish graduated from McGill University in the late 1960's with both civil law and common law degrees. He is the senior partner in his law firm, Fish & Associates, which he established in 1973. He is a member of the Society of Trust and Estate Practitioners and has a lengthy experience in the field of estate disputes. Barry is a co-author of The Family Fight... Planning to Avoid it, The Family War...Winning the Inheritance Battle, and Where There's an Inheritance, Stories from Inside the World of Two Wills Lawyers.

He is a frequent radio and television guest, and a contributor to various newspapers and magazines, including Good Housekeeping. He was host of the Protect Yourself radio show, and a frequent guest on the Money Line television show. He has, as well, been a guest on CTV News. He is married and has two children and three grandchildren. His firm's website is www.familyfight.com. Barry can be reached at bfish@fishlaw.ca.

Les Kotzer has been a wills lawyer since 1989. He graduated law school on the Dean's List. He is a member of the Society of Trust and Estate Practitioners. In 2013, he was awarded the Queen's Elizabeth II Diamond Jubilee Medal for his work in simplifying this complex area of law for the public. He is co-author of The Family Fight...Planning to Avoid it, The Family War...Winning the Inheritance Battle, and Where There's an Inheritance, Stories from Inside the World of Two Wills Lawyers.

Les is also a regular guest on television and radio shows across North America. He has appeared on CITY TV, CTV News, CNN, and Fox News. He has also been featured in publications across North America including Time Magazine, Newsweek, Fortune Magazine, Money Magazine, Good Housekeeping, The Wall Street Journal, The National Post, the Globe and Mail, U.S.A. Today, and The New York Times. His website is www.leskotzer.com.

Les is also a professional songwriter. He has written the lyrics for the songs on the CD entitled "A Family United, A Family Divided." Three of his songs, "These are our Heroes," "You Made a Difference," and "Photos in a Drawer," can be heard on various radio stations. He has a second website devoted to his songs: www.songwritinglawyer.com. Les can be reached at leskotzer@familyfight.com.

ACKNOWLEDGEMENTS

Even when a book is written by co-authors, the act of writing is a very lonely experience. Time swallows the minutes and the hours. The computer screen seems to be the only landscape. The comfort is that we were not really alone in the process of writing this book. Those who supported us in so many ways during the writing of this book are the staff at our office, being Benedetta, Robyn, and Risa. We also thank Melissa Benchetrit, whose art work appears on our book cover, and our very close friends, Louis Manne and Wendy Watson, who gave us their help and support. Those who inspired us are our families, and, to them we devote the remaining words of this acknowledgment:

BARRY M. FISH

At the time of the first printing of this book, my mother is now 99. I wrote about her when our book entitled, Where There's an Inheritance, was about to be printed. I love her dearly.

My wife, Pearl, has been an excellent support for me. She has been a patient wife on those long days when I would come home late for supper because Les and I were working on this book.

My biggest fans are my children, Joanna and Adrian. As they grow and mature, I hope to have three new fans in my two granddaughters, Nadia and Tamara, and also in my new grandson, Adam.

When I wrote my acknowledgements for Where There's an Inheritance, I mentioned these words about my late father, Abe, and they are worth repeating here: "The words in this book will never pass before his eyes, but it is in the words of this book that his inspiration will live."

LES KOTZER

The inspiration from my late mother, Rose, and my late father, Jack, is big part of my life. Not a day goes by that I don't think of them. They weren't just my parents; they were my best friends. No words can express my thanks for all that they have done for me. I have always aspired to conduct myself the way I know they expected of me. In 2012, I lost my younger brother Joel, who was the best brother anyone could ever have. I loved him so much, and no words can describe how much I miss him.

My wife, Miriam, is a beautiful person inside and out. When I met her in 1980, I never dreamt that someone could have such a positive impact on my life. She is my strength. She is always there for me. I love her dearly.

My loving daughters, Suzie and Michelle, have accomplished so much in their careers as young lawyers. They are my treasures; and, I cannot imagine a father being more proud of his daughters, or loving them any more than I love both of them.

My family means everything to me.

DEDICATION
For:
Miriam, Suzie, and Michelle
Pearl, Joanna, Adrian, Nadia, Tamara, and baby Adam

THE WILLS LAWYERS: THEIR STORIES OF:
Money, inheritance, greed, family and... BETRAYAL

TABLE OF CONTENTS

I often see siblings fighting over their late parents' estates. I wrote this song about two imaginary brothers at war over their mother's estate. I wanted to show through song what can happen to families.

Les Kotzer

THE FAMILY FIGHT SONG

We're dividing all of Mother's things
Deciding on her rugs and rings
I can't believe what's happening tonight
We're in a family fight

Can't split a painting on the wall
Or share a table in the hall
I never dreamt that we could fall apart
It would break our mother's heart

What kind of message does this send?
My brother, always my best friend
Do hurting hearts ever mend?
Or is this how our story ends?

Tonight
We're in a family fight
As kids
We'd talk away the night
But now
We're in a family fight

We don't see this working out
His lawyer called today
Look how fast our lives can change
What would mother say?

I never thought that I would see
These winds destroy our family tree
Memories are drifting in the storm
Those frozen moments always kept me warm

As kids
We'd talk away the night
But now
We're in a family fight

Lyrics by Les Kotzer
Music by Lewis Manne
Produced by Wendy Watson
© 2004 Manimal Music and Lesko Music
Hear the song on www.touchyourheartsongs.com

INTRODUCTION

We hope you will enjoy reading this book. Some of the stories may shock you; some may make you angry; others may touch your heart; and, some of the stories may make you smile or even laugh. We have co-authored three other books, entitled The Family Fight, The Family War (with Jordan Atin, a certified specialist in estates and trusts law) and, Where There's an Inheritance. In each of these books, you will find many stories from inside our world of working with people as they prepare their wills, execute the wills of others, and, navigate through the myriad of complications involving money, inheritance, greed, family, and betrayal. Our previous books have been featured in major media outlets across North America, and each book has drawn enthusiastic response from the public at large. We have written this fourth book to address innumerable requests for even more stories from our world.

It appears to us that a large segment of the public wants a glimpse into the world of wills and estates. This is a world that few people have a chance to view from a close perspective. We have repeatedly been told that we get to see the very best and the very worst of humankind. True enough, we have been fortunate to witness the best in people. Some of the touching stories in this book reflect deep love, gentle kindness, and self-less generosity. But when it comes to the other extreme of humankind, some of the stories in this book are dredged from the depths of that world, fuelled by money, family discord, greed, and betrayal.

The inheritance-related stories you will read in this book are based on our many and collective years in the field of wills and estates. Our personal experiences have been varied. We have met many individuals in many walks of life who have had interesting and important stories to tell. We have listened intently to each of them. Similarly, we have lent a sensitive ear to participants at our seminars, callers on our TV and radio shows, and other professionals in the field of wills and estates who we have met. Each person, in his or her own way, contributed to our ability to put these stories in writing.

Some of the stories in our book are based on situations where we are obliged to respect lawyer-client confidentiality. Wherever a story in our book makes reference to a client who has come to our office, we have deliberately removed all

of the detail which is traceable to any of the parties involved, or their families, their businesses, or their personal affairs. Nothing in our book can be traced directly or indirectly to any client of ours. We have, where necessary, varied the information involved so that no description of what you will read in this book can lead to the identity of any person. In all of our stories, what we intend to share with the reader is the emotional impact of the situations they each have brought before us. Moments frozen in time have been preserved, and it is around these precious and fleeting experiences that the stories have been compiled.
If there is one phrase to express the intention of our book, it is that the reader benefit in his or her own life by the lessons to be learned in reading these stories.

Finally, what we wish to share with you is this: while rules of protocol and professionalism may restrain the hand that writes and the lips that speak, nothing can restrain what lies in the hearts of those who have a message that yearns to be set free. Many of these stories have had a permanent impact on us, and we believe that they will have an impact on you.

*"In business circles, my big-shot brother likes to be referred to
by his first and middle names... Randall Quincey...
but at home we just call him "Owen"...
because he's always in debt, and owin' money to everybody..."*

1. TAKING DAD FOR A RIDE

Stan, an accountant by profession, had, at first, very much appreciated the efforts of his brother, Charlie. Their mother had passed away, leaving behind the two of them and their frail, 89-year-old father, Leland. Most of Stan's time was spent by having to work hard at the office; but Charlie, who had taken an early retirement from his job, spent a great deal of his time with their father, Leland. Stan was impressed with Charlie's dedication to their father. Wherever Charlie went, Leland was invited. Without exception, whether it was a restaurant, or a trip, if Charlie was there, so was Leland. Leland had mild dementia, so Stan felt very comforted that his brother was so involved in the life of their frail, elderly father.

Stan was also impressed that Charlie had organized all of his vacations so that Leland would be included along with Charlie's own family - Charlie's wife and their teen-aged boys.

Stan's initial impressions changed almost immediately after Leland's last trip to Florida. Leland passed away two weeks after they returned. Stan was the sole executor of Leland's estate.

As he began the estate administration, Stan's admiration for his brother, Charlie, began to melt away, and eventually turned to disgust. In point form, this is what destroyed Stan's relationship with Charlie.

Point 1: Leland's last credit card bill came to Stan about ten days after the funeral. The bill exceeded $30,000 for a ten-day trip. Not only did it show payment for the vacation Charlie took to Disneyworld with his wife and two teen-aged boys, the vacation included payment for water skiing, surf boarding lessons, shopping at exclusive stores and boutiques, and an evening at a very expensive club.

Point 2: Not only was it offensive that it was Leland's credit card that paid for all of this, but it was all the more infuriating when one realized that Leland was 89 years old, walked with a walker, and had mild dementia.

Point 3: As Stan acquired more and more paperwork, he realized that the only reason for Leland to be present when Charlie entertained himself and his family was the fact that every vacation, every restaurant, and every flight, was paid for by Leland's credit card.

When Stan investigated more deeply into Leland's financial records, he saw clearly that, further back in time, Leland's credit card had paid for sailing, scuba diving, skiing, wine tasting tours and the like.

Point 4: Stan could only imagine his late father being dragged along to some club or restaurant while Charlie, his wife, and kids lived it up. Then he imagined Charlie taking his father's hand to help Leland sign the credit card slips. In all likelihood, Leland had no idea what he was paying. And all these bills were paid out of Leland's accounts at his bank. He wondered if a trip to Leland's bank was among the trips that Charlie took with Dad.

"My brother had pulled the wool over my eyes and my Dad's eyes ever since my Mom died; but now I see that bloodsucker for which he really is. It wasn't my Dad who Charlie cared about…it was my Dad's credit card!"

2. THE HEIR CUTS

After deferring for over fifteen years to revise her will, Maureen finally decided to take steps to move forward and update her will. Her old will left everything to her four children equally; but now, she was cutting out three of them and leaving everything to her youngest daughter, Amy.

Maureen had this to say about her four children:

"My husband died; and my daughter, Chelsea, didn't come to the funeral. She said she couldn't get a flight out. But if that's the case, she still could have come a few days later. She never came. I think she didn't come because she had something more important in her life…her bridge club. I tried to forgive her, but I can't.

I went through a serious operation, and my son, Brahm, never visited me in the hospital. Not once. He never even called me. I guess he likes the sun, and it's too cold up here. He must have been too busy with his golf clubs to think of me. I tried to forgive him, but I can't.

During the summer, I had a complicated move to my retirement home. But my daughter, Crystal, who lives close by, never lifted a finger to help me. At the same time, my brother died. Crystal was nowhere to be found. She must have been at her yacht club. I tried to forgive her, but I can't.

The only one of my children who was always there for me is my youngest, Amy. I don't know what I would do without her. She deserves to get everything that I own.

After I die, I don't care if people look at me as a bad mother. Yes, I do love all of my kids. But I just don't like three of them!"

3. A FRANK DISCUSSION

Rosa came into my office for a review of her will. She put the sealed envelope containing her will down on the boardroom table in front of me. She sarcastically commented that the only reason she was in my office, was that her friend told her that someone should take a look at her will, just in case. She told me that she thought that her will was perfect, and that she was just wasting her time with this appointment.

I opened the envelope and took out the will to read through it. It was a home-made will, typed, dated, and signed with two witnesses. Also, her will was a very lengthy document. I looked, page-after-page, for the part of the will which named her executor and beneficiaries. Finally, on page eight, I landed on the part that concluded my quick search.

After reading her entire will, I looked up at her and saw that she was reaching for her coat. "See? I told you there was nothing wrong with it," she said. I responded with the following comment. "You told me your husband had passed away. The way I read your will, it appears that you have one child." She said, "No! What are you talking about? I have three! And, I love them all! Why would you ask me that?" I responded that the will I had just read had named her son, Frank, as her only executor and the only beneficiary of her estate.

"I haven't read through my whole will, but I'm sure you're reading it wrong!" she quickly retorted. "I want Frank as my only executor, but everything I own goes equally to all three kids." I turned the will around and asked her to look at the paragraph that I was looking at which was buried deep into the document. That paragraph said, "I love my son Frank so much. He is the best son in the world. There is no other child like him. I want him to get the residue of my estate." She then asked what the "residue" of her estate meant. I explained that it meant everything left in her estate after the payment of her debts and taxes. She looked at me, stared, and seemed frozen in her seat. Now her coat was back on the chair beside her.

"Where did you get this will?" I asked. "It was from a form we got from the Internet," she replied. Now she was concerned, and said that she was not familiar with legal language, and that she had no idea that her will cut out her other two children, leaving everything to Frank. "I can't figure out what went wrong," she said.

When I asked her who typed this will for her, she looked down at the floor, her face turning red with embarrassment, and said, "Frank did."

4. THE SACRED PROMISE

Lucy and Domenica were Janice's only children. For the purpose of this story, we will refer to Janice as "Mom." Over the years, Mom was a single mother and struggled to raise them. Although they were fortunate enough to live in the small house that Dad had left to Mom, times were never easy; and Mom had made numerous trips to the Food Bank to tide over the little family.

As time went on, Lucy and Domenica got their education and found good jobs. They were able to contribute to the household; and eventually, with their efforts, somehow surmounted the bad times. Mom was able to keep the little house; but she never forgot how the Food Bank had saved them through those formative years.

Just after Lucy got married, Mom became terminally ill. Domenica looked after Mom for the six months before Mom went to the palliative care section of the hospital. At this point, Mom knew that she did not have long to live; and she asked both of her daughters to come there together, because she had something important to tell them.

In her hospital bed, and with the two girls at her bedside, Mom spoke of a serious mistake she had made, and she asked the girls to promise that they would make it right. "I was up all night because I realized that I had made a mistake in my will and I didn't want to die before I corrected it. And now, I am not strong enough to get involved with a lawyer to make a new will. When I made my will, I left everything to the two of you girls, but I forgot one important thing. The Food Bank saved our lives. They put a roof over our heads. They saved Christmas for both of you when you were young. They deserve to be in my will, but it's too late for me now. Please promise me that you will give the Food Bank a $15,000 donation in my name, after I am gone. Once you make that promise to me, I'll be able to sleep."

Both girls took Mom's hand, promising that they would do what Mom asked. They assured Mom that she would have nothing to worry about. Lucy said, "How can we not follow your wishes, Mom? The Food Bank was our guardian angel."

It was not very long before Mom passed away. Domenica was the executor named in Mom's will. In the course of arranging the affairs of Mom's estate, she called her sister, Lucy, to bring her up-to-date on the financial matters. One of the points she raised in her call to Lucy was about the $15,000 donation she was going to send to the Food Bank.

Lucy's response: "What are you talking about? There's nothing in the will except that you and I will divide Mom's estate equally between the two of us. There's nothing about the Food Bank in Mom's will."

Domenica reminded her sister about their promise to Mom when they were at her bedside, and the peace that they had brought to Mom by promising her that they would not let her down, and that the mistake she made in her will would be repaired by them. She reminded Lucy about her comment to Mom about the Food Bank being their guardian angel.

Lucy: "That was all an act to make Mom happy. I will not allow you to use estate money, half of which belongs to me, for a gift to the Food Bank. If you do, I will hire a lawyer and will sue you for not following what Mom's will says."

Domenica: "How dare you talk like that? How greedy can you be? If that's how you feel, I don't want to talk to you ever again. So from now on, everything between us will only be in writing. How soon we forget!"

From the legal point of view, Lucy got her way. Domenica didn't want a lawsuit. After a year of utter silence between the now-estranged sisters, the estate, in fact, was split equally between them, exactly as Lucy had demanded. But there is more to this story than the legal aspect. With her inheritance in hand, Domenica then took it upon herself to donate $15,000 of her own money to the Food Bank in Mom's name. Along with the donation, Domenica sent a handwritten note stating that, years ago, the Food Bank had saved Mom, herself, and her sister from disaster. The note and the accompanying donation were being made in the memory of a once-poor, young mother named Janice, who was a regular dependant, and whose name was probably long-forgotten. In preparing this emotional letter, Domenica made mention of a young volunteer whose name was Margaret, and who always had a smile for their mother, Janice.

Domenica's note ended with a heartfelt thanks for the Food Bank's helping hand extended to Janice so very many years ago. So much time had passed since the days that Mom was at the Food Bank, that Domenica's note was not addressed to anyone in particular.

It was, therefore, a pleasant shock to Domenica to find the following handwritten response attached to the tax receipt that was sent to her in the postal mail:

"I am so sorry to hear that Janice has passed. She was a proud lady, beautiful inside and out. I remember her vividly, coming in with her two little girls. I remember Janice telling me, more than once, that the day would come when she would climb out of her temporary problems and then she could dress her two princesses in something better than the hand-me-downs they wore. And, I always had an extra cookie or two for each of Janice's little girls. I remember how Janice couldn't stop thanking me for making their faces light up with those cookies. Janice may have had a hard life, but I am touched that she remembered us after so many years. Her donation will make other little faces light up in the years to come. Love...Margaret."

Domenica lost no time in sending a copy of Margaret's letter to sister Lucy, who she hadn't spoken to since Lucy broke her promise to Mom. The only words Domenica had for her sister were, "Hope you're enjoying your money. I sent my own money to the Food Bank on Mom's behalf. At least one of us respected Mom's last wishes. And remember, Margaret? The Food Bank volunteer that Mom always talked about and called 'Sweet Margaret'? That nice girl who slipped us those extra cookies when we were there with Mom? Well, she still remembers where you came from, even if you don't!"

5. THE HUG FACTOR

Archie and Matilda were in my office to speak about their wills. They were in their early seventies, very astute, and extremely wealthy. They wanted to leave their estates to one another, and then they were thinking of dividing their estates equally among their children after both of them had passed away.

When I asked if they had grandchildren, I had inadvertently triggered an argument between the two of them.

Archie explained that they had three grandchildren, all of whom were hard-working, young adults in their late twenties. He then looked at me and said, "I don't think we should leave them any money in our wills. I think we should give them a good sum, like $25,000.00 each, to help them out now."

Matilda turned to Archie. "No, Archie, I disagree. We're going to spoil them. Let them learn responsibility by working for their money. They can get our money after we die. Let's leave the amount you want to give them in our wills."

Archie met these comments with silence. I could see his face harden. He pushed back his chair and walked out, leaving me alone in the boardroom with Matilda. Sensing a looming conflict, I excused myself and went out to the parking lot, where I saw Archie pacing. I asked if we could work out some resolution to the issue. He agreed and came back in.

As soon as he entered the boardroom, Matilda met him with a cold stare. But everything changed with what Archie had to say. "Teaching them responsibility is important; but seeing the smiles in their eyes when we give them the money is important, as well. If we leave the money in our wills, they'll get it; and I am sure they'll be thankful after we both die. But if we give them the money now, when they really need it, and when it will solve many problems for them, what we will get will be warm hugs and kisses from them. So, Matilda, what I'm saying is this: If we give them the money now, we get a hug and a kiss, and we'll have the enjoyment of seeing them benefit from our hard work. If we leave it to them in our wills, we get nothing back from them when they get it. We'll be dead."

Hearing that, Matilda smiled at Archie, grabbed his hand and said, "Archie, you're right."

6. THE BANK OF MOM & DAD

Martin, Sonya, and Andre always got what they wanted from Mom and Dad. Football, baseball, dance lessons, and innumerable other after-school activities were always paid fully and happily by Mom and Dad. When the kids were young, they were easy to spoil, and spoiled they were.

However, as time went on, so did the expenses of Martin, Sonya, and Andre. Martin's expenses did not match Sonya's; and Sonya's expenses paled in comparison to Andre's. One child went to the community college in town; one child went to a university close to town; and one child went to pursue a post-graduate degree out of the country.

All of these expenses were paid by Mom and Dad, who paid out of love, and who never counted which child got more than the others. Unlike some of the kids' friends, who had to work part-time jobs to pay their own way, Mom and Dad never expected their kids to pay their own expenses.

Everything changed when Martin had to ask Mom and Dad for financial help for his upcoming wedding. When Dad asked Martin what his future in-laws were contributing, Martin reacted angrily. "What about Sonya's car? What about Andre's college tuition?"

Mom and Dad were shocked that their generosity had created problems; and, they immediately called a meeting with all three children.

"We want to be upfront with you, and, we don't want you kids to ever fight with each other over money. We called this meeting because Martin wants us to pay for part of his wedding, and we want to help him out. We always want to be open with all of you."

Martin exclaimed, "What do you mean PART of the wedding? I thought you were going to pay for the WHOLE thing? If YOU don't pay for it, then who else is going to pay for it?"

His brother, Andre's, reaction was: "If Martin gets all that money for his wedding, then I want the same amount, too! I signed up to go to the Antarctic, and that trip is going to cost big bucks!"

Sonya looked at Mom. "You bought each of my brothers a new suit for their graduations but you never bought me a prom dress."

Accusations led to bursts of angry reactions, Mom started to cry; and then it was Dad's turn to react; and, he did so very angrily. "No wedding money, no trip money, no more money for anyone! We spoiled you rotten! Now all that's going to change. You're on your own. Our meeting is over."

And with the meeting now over, the kids, scowling and arguing, went out the front door, followed by Dad. As they turned to look back at Dad, he hollered, "Start making your own money because Mom and Dad's bank is closed. Forever!"

7. IT'S MY MONEY NOW

Jordana wanted to know whether she could sue her father, Richard. I could tell by her mood that she was holding back a fair amount of anger. This was the story that led to her appointment with me.

Her late grandparents were hard-working people, who had accumulated several properties over many years. After her grandmother passed away, Jordana's grandfather became very close to her. They used to spend a great deal of time together, and their friendship was very special. She called him "Grandpa" and he called her "my precious Jordi." Jordana became emotional as she explained to me how Grandpa took her into his confidence, even more than he did with his only child, Jordana's mother.

Grandpa told Jordana how hard he had to work to build his wealth. He started working day and night to clean offices. Some nights he slept on the floors that he had just finished cleaning. He eventually had enough money saved to buy and renovate a house; and from there, he built up everything he owned with his own two hands. He would consistently tell Jordana that all that he had would one day be hers. He was going to leave his substantial estate to Jordana's mother, and he was sure that when she passed away, she would leave everything to Jordana. More than once, Grandpa told Jordana that she would one day benefit from all of his hard work. She repeated Grandpa's statement, "What did I work so hard for, if not to share it with the ones I love?"

Over the years that passed, Grandpa would help his precious Jordi with generous birthday presents, all of her school tuition and fees, and Grandpa even bought her the first car she owned.

When Grandpa passed away, Jordana was devastated, as was her mother. However, Jordana's misery did not end there. Within a few months after Grandpa's estate was settled, her mother had a fatal heart attack, and now there was a second funeral.

Her dad, Richard, shared Jordana's pain over their loss. They acted on advice to join a support group, which offered grief counseling, and met every Wednesday night for a number of months. During that time, there were no secrets between Jordana and her dad, Richard. He explained to Jordana that her mom's will had left everything she owned, to him.

After several grief counseling sessions, Jordana introduced her father to Lucy, who Jordana had befriended, and who was also a member of their support group. Lucy was an attractive lady who had tragically lost her husband in an industrial accident. Like Jordana, she had joined this support group for help with their grief over the loss of a significant loved one. Lucy was about twenty years younger than Richard. Also, she had twins who were thirteen years old.

Richard, Jordana, and Lucy became close to one another and were, in a way, a group within that support group. When, ultimately, there were no more sessions to attend, the three of them continued to get together socially. Just as it looked as if

Jordana had a new friend in Lucy, things began to change. Richard would not be home for supper, leaving Jordana to eat alone. Richard would be away on weekends, and always the reason was Lucy. Furthermore, the short friendship that had begun to form between Lucy and Jordana seemed to come to an end, as Lucy stopped calling Jordana; and when Jordana called Lucy, it seemed as if Jordana had to climb over obstacles to get her on the phone. This was especially frustrating because Jordana had lost her job, and this was getting her down. At least she had Richard's roof over her head, although Richard still seemed to be tight financially. Where was all the money?

After a few months, Richard had "exciting" news for Jordana. He had given Lucy a diamond ring for their engagement, and was going to sell the house and buy a more expensive one because he and Lucy felt it was best for the twins to be brought up in a larger and more comfortable home. At this time, Jordana had news for Richard. She told him that she had a great opportunity to buy a small clothing boutique, and, with a decent down payment, she would be able to buy the business, and she wouldn't have to worry about looking for a job anymore. What was Richard's response to her? "We'd better talk."

This was not the answer that Jordana expected from her father. But it got worse. First of all, Richard said that he just couldn't give her that down payment. When she pressed him for a reason, Richard explained that new responsibilities came along with his new family. The twins would need more than just a new home. Richard would be facing fees for their private school and summer camp; and he would have to save for their future university education. As well, he had to consider the significant overhead of a larger home.

Jordana was stunned by his response and she was seething. She said it was impossible for her to live in the same house as Lucy and her teenaged twins. She wanted to know what Richard was going to do about it. After all, she was unemployed, and the only opportunity she saw to move ahead in her life was the very business that Richard now refused her his help. The most Richard would do for her was to help her with rent on an apartment, if she insisted on living on her own.

She retorted, "Look, Dad, you are using the money you inherited from Mom. This was Grandpa's hard-earned money, the money he promised that would help me in my life." Richard's response, the arrogant response that was placing Jordana in front of my desk, was simple: "Well, I don't care if it was once Grandpa's money; and I don't care what he promised you. It's my money now; and I can do what I want with it. If you don't like it, leave, and don't be surprised if I cut you out of my will."

As I looked at Jordana, her face flushed with the rage which was being unleashed in this meeting with me. Her final comments were, "Grandpa would be sick and horrified if he knew that everything he had worked for would go to people who were not even related to him."

8. MY BROTHER, THE CON MAN

In our jurisdiction, it is rare to see creditors attend a preliminary bankruptcy meeting. But in the case of Simon, the bankrupt, he had fooled so many people, and was so detested, that there were two dozen creditors attending this bankruptcy meeting. This is where I met Jenna, as both of us had claims against Simon. Jenna related the following story to me.

Simon was Jenna's brother. Over a number of years, he had "borrowed" a considerable sum of money from their mother. He had also borrowed heavily from Jenna. Simon never paid back one cent to either of them. He was such a rogue that Holly-Ann, his wife of twenty years, could no longer stand him; and she had left him the previous year.

Jenna was not painting a very pretty picture of Simon; but with the next part of Jenna's story, my impression of Simon began to darken even further.

Jenna told me the following about a recent discussion she had with Holly-Ann, Simon's now-separated wife. Holly-Ann spoke of the bracelet which Jenna's and

Simon's mother used to wear with pride. It was an expensive, 18-karat, gold bracelet which had inlaid emeralds and diamonds. She had kept it in a special, wooden box, and only wore it on very special occasions. It had been left to Jenna in their mother's will, along with all of her mother's other jewelry. After their mother passed away, Simon, who was their mother's executor, handed over to Jenna, all of their mother's jewelry, all contained in this wooden box. Jenna then placed all of her inherited jewelry in her safety deposit box.

However, Simon had shared a secret with Holly-Ann during the time they were still happily married, and living together. Simon had told Holly-Ann of his visit to his mother's apartment at a time when she was in a convalescent home. He let himself into her apartment and "borrowed" the bracelet, taking it from its wooden box. Then Simon paid a visit to a friend of his who was a jeweler. Simon asked his friend the jeweler to make a copy of this bracelet, duplicating its appearance, but using 10-karat gold with cheap stones that resembled emeralds and diamonds. The jeweler made the cheap duplicate bracelet very quickly. Before Simon's mother returned to her apartment from the convalescent home, Simon put the imitation jewelry back in the wooden box. No one was the wiser. His mother never knew the difference, nor did Jenna, at the time. He then sold the real bracelet for serious money in order to pay off some of his own debts.

Simon had threatened Holly-Ann to never tell a soul about what he had done with his mother's bracelet. It would be their secret "or else." But after their bitter separation, Holly-Ann could not wait to broadcast to anyone would listen, and especially to Jenna, the sordid details which would show what a scoundrel and a cheat Simon was.

When Jenna heard this story from Holly-Ann about the bracelet, she could hardly believe that even a fraudster as bad as her brother would stoop to such depths. So, just to check out Holly-Ann's story, she took the bracelet she had inherited from her mother out of the safety deposit box. She went downtown to the jewelry appraiser who examined the bracelet and confirmed Holly-Ann's story.
Yes, indeed, the bracelet was 10-karat gold instead of 18-karat gold. Furthermore, it was indeed inlaid with cheap stones and broken glass. The bracelet was, essentially, costume jewelry. As the jewelry appraiser told her, "This piece is practically worthless."

This trickery and betrayal by her now-bankrupt brother was what brought Jenna to this creditor's meeting. Just as Holly-Ann had been so ready to tell the worst about her husband she had separated from, Jenna was now ready to do the same to him, even if he was her brother. After all, didn't everyone deserve to know the truth? Jenna told us that she could not wait to repeat this story to the group. "After this," she said, "I plan to tell the whole world."

9. UNCLE MO'S DOUGH

Howie was Uncle Mo's executor and he was furious when he came in my office to deal with Uncle Mo's estate. In order to understand Howie's anger, you have to know the family situation. Howie was the only child of Sybil, Uncle Mo's sole-surviving sibling.

Howie's Mom, Sybil, had always been extremely close to her brother, Mo. She was there for him every time Mo had to go to the hospital; and she had lost count of the number of times she had spent the night at Mo's bedside. Sybil was a dedicated and loyal sister.

During the years that Mo's health was declining, Sybil had lost her husband; and before many years had passed, she found herself not only widowed, but with very little income. The burden of looking after Sybil had gradually shifted to Howie who had to thinly stretch his finances. Howie did not have much money, but he loved his mother, Sybil, and wanted her to have the best life she could.

Therefore, with Howie's help, Sybil lived in a nice retirement home. However, the monthly fees had drained all of her money long ago, and, now those fees were choking Howie so badly that he had to put a new mortgage on his own home. Howie's wife went along with this, but to say she was displeased would be a gross understatement.

THE WILLS LAWYERS: THEIR STORIES OF:
Money, inheritance, greed, family and... BETRAYAL

When Uncle Mo died, he was an eighty-year-old bachelor with no children.
His will cut his only sister, Sybil, totally out of his estate, which was worth about
$800,000. Every cent of it went to charity. Mo's estate could have provided
desperately-needed financial relief to Howie, if Mo's will had left at least some of
his money to Sybil. The money could have been used to look after her. The fact
that Sybil was cut out of her brother Mo's will ensured that Howie would be
indebted for the rest of Sybil's life, and beyond.

At first, Howie just could not believe that his uncle would betray his mother this
way. But what turned Howie's disbelief to fury was the letter that Uncle Mo left
with his will.

Paraphrasing Mo's letter: "Sybil, you are a wonderful sister. I love you. To pay
tribute for all you have done for me, I am leaving my entire estate to a charity so
that I can help many people who are hard of hearing like you are. I know that you
don't need my money. You would probably be insulted if I left you money because
your husband was a proud, self-made, wealthy man. I am sure he left you well-
protected."

Enraged, Howie blasted out, "Uncle Mo was wrong. My Dad was not a wealthy
man. As a matter of fact, he never had money, and he fooled Uncle Mo just like he
fooled everyone else."

Howie's father's high-living, free-spending lifestyle had misled Uncle Mo; and
therefore, created Mo's impression that Sybil was a wealthy woman.

The reality was that Howie's father always smoked a large cigar, belonged to a
prestigious golf club, and drove a convertible. He constantly bragged of his exotic
travels and of his shrewd investments. But all of this was a facade. Howie's father
was a dreamer, in debt, and heavily-mortgaged. When he passed away, he had left
Sybil practically impoverished.

Looking back on Howie's story, we wonder about his enraged feelings toward
Uncle Mo. Was Uncle Mo more to blame than Howie's father? All we know is that
if both men had realized how their beloved sister and wife would have ended up,
they would have probably done things very differently. Now, it was up to Howie to
spend the rest of his years, doing without, in order to take care of his mother.

10. GOIN' OUT IN STYLE

We were at a lunchtime workshop for a local company where we were invited to speak to a staff of about fifty people on the subject of wills. That same company also invited a funeral director and we shared the question-and-answer session with him. It did not take long for the participants to come up with some interesting questions, as well as some strange personal stories. Of all of those stories, we would like to share the one told by Denise.

Her uncle's real name has to remain a secret, but she did say that it was a lot longer than his nickname, "Lefty." Denise began to describe him by putting this comment to her co-workers: "If you imagine what a rich person looks like, you will see Lefty." She spoke of the quality of his suits, shirts, ties, and shoes. She described the Cadillac he drove. She continued a bit longer with the image of a wealthy executive, then began to describe the life her uncle really lived.

Lefty had many friends, and loved to party; but Lefty was a gambler, and an awful one at that. His only homes were cheap hotel rooms; and when, from time-to-time, he totally ran out of money, he slept on a couch in a back room at her father's office. Lefty's Armani's suit impressed his friends, and his Canali suit impressed those who held his gambling debts. However, what they didn't know was that Lefty was exactly the same size as Denise's father, who gave Lefty generous access to whatever was hanging in his closet. The shiny car Lefty drove was leased, and paid for by her father, who could afford it because he happened to be a truly wealthy man. Brotherly love was the only currency that ended up in Lefty's pocket.

His "friends" included those to whom he owed money for his gambling debts.

True to form, when Lefty passed away, Denise's father paid for a large and lavish funeral. As the many mourners paid their respects, Denise repeatedly overheard how impressed they were with Lefty's wealth, his accomplishments, even the richness of the ceremony and the funeral reception.

Shortly after Lefty's funeral, Denise's father passed away. He may have been wealthy, but he was a humble man; and his humility found expression in the simplicity of his own funeral. Unlike the rich, wood-grained, and brass-handled casket that held Lefty's body, Denise's father was buried in an unpainted pine coffin in a simple, graveside funeral.

Many of the same people who paid their respects to Denise at her father's funeral, had also previously attended Lefty's funeral. She could not help overhearing them compare the two funerals; and some of them even spoke of the way that the funerals of the rich were so different from the funerals of those who weren't. Of all of the comments she heard from Lefty's friends and acquaintances, the statement that made Denise stand up to tell her story was the one which contained the ultimate irony: "Too bad he couldn't have made it the way Lefty did."

She finished her story with these words: "I never embarrassed Uncle Lefty, not even after he passed away; but some of his friends will learn the truth when they start looking for his gambling debts to be paid back."

11. WAITING FOR THOSE WORDS

This is a story about a well-known person who would be easily recognized in his field, having won many awards. With his work, he has touched the hearts and minds of the public. This celebrity was in his sixties when I first met with him.

When he came in for his appointment, the first thing he asked was how long the appointment might last. He told me that his 95-year-old mother was in the car, and he did not want her to sit alone for a prolonged period of time. I told him that we would be about a half-hour. He then asked me if his mother could come in from the car to wait in our waiting room while I met with him to sign his will. I told him that she certainly could and that it would be my pleasure to meet her.

As he helped her to get seated in the waiting room, I turned to her and said she must be so proud of such an accomplished and talented son. She looked at him, and then at me. She smiled and said, "Yes. I am REALLY proud of him. He is very special."

Then he came with me into the boardroom. Before I started to explain his will to him, I could see his eyes were tearing and that he was clearly emotional. He then said that he wanted to thank me so much for what I just had just done. However, I did not realize what I had done that deserved such thanks. "You got my mom to say something that I have been waiting for her to say all of my life…that she is really proud of me." He went on to explain that since his late teens, his mother had always told him that he was a dreamer, just wasting his time, that he was heading in the wrong direction with his career, and that he should be looking for a "real" job. He shared with me, "When I started to win various awards, she would tell me that I was just a flash in the pan, and that there was no future in what I was doing. It was devastating to hear this from my own mother; but I wouldn't give up.

You have to know that what motivated me for so much of my career, more than the awards, more than the accolades, and more than the money, was my yearning to hear my Mom say the words I have just heard. Nothing means more to me. I finally feel good inside."

I was surprised when he made this comment. It seemed natural to me for a mother to praise her son for his accomplishments - especially the accomplishments recognized by so many people, and on such a high magnitude of respect.

After his will was signed and witnessed, I walked back to the waiting room with him, to say "good-bye" to his mother. He hugged her, and told her how much he loved her. She said to him, "I love you, too. You know I've always been so proud of you, don't you?"

You never fully know what resides deep inside a person, even an accomplished celebrity such as this man. Surely, he had won the hearts of so many fans, yet he was thirsting his entire professional life for the recognition from one particular person.

This is just another example that the very thing we think a person is striving to achieve, may not be the money or fame that he or she is receiving. In this man's case, it was his mother's acceptance of his career choice and the recognition that he had done well.

12. HOME

Vincenzo and his brother, both in their fifties, came into my office because their mother had recently passed away. They were now having to focus on looking after her estate matters. They had brought her important papers to me in a thick file folder. I pulled a will out of the folder which, upon a first reading, had totally excluded Vincenzo. A letter accompanied that will which indicated that Vincenzo had been excluded because of his estrangement from the family. I then had to ask Vincenzo to leave the room, as he was not involved in the estate. But his brother said, "No! Momma made another will that changed everything, once Vincenzo came back into our family!" Sure enough, I looked through the folder and found a more recent will. Vincenzo was not only included as beneficiary of half of the estate, but was also named as co-executor with his brother.

Lawyers are always concerned about changes of this sort, because we want to ensure that changes to a will are voluntary, and are not brought about by undue influence on the person who is making the will. But Vincenzo's brother was the only other heir to the estate; and he was right there to assure me that the changes to their mother's will were perfectly voluntary and that there was no undue influence exerted on her at all to change her will.

The subject of Vincenzo's estrangement from the family had an emotional effect on him. He told me that it tears at his heart to think about what he did to his family. At this point in our conversation, Vincenzo felt that he owed an explanation and wished to talk about what drove him away from the family, and what eventually drew him back into it.

As a twenty-year-old rebel, Vincenzo left the household to live his own life. Life with his brother and parents had left him frustrated, bored, and hostile. He could not see the point to the type of lives they all lived, and he did not care or understand it. They seemed to be pushing him to an education which he did not want, and one which he felt was useless. What had appealed to Vincenzo was a night life, as well as a life of hard drinking and partying. He became a drifter of sorts, and the only contact he maintained with the family was through his brother, who would exchange phone calls with him once every two or three weeks.

One of these calls from his brother came to Vincenzo about seven years ago, when his brother telephoned in a panic to tell him that their father was very sick in the hospital, and that he might even be on his deathbed. Was this an exaggeration? It would be up to Vincenzo to believe his brother and show up at the hospital or to just let things go. It had been over thirty years since he last saw his father.

Vincenzo decided to show up at the hospital. However, his attitude about this visit was very negative. He felt that he would be going through a totally useless exercise, a complete waste of time. Furthermore, Vincenzo had no idea what he would say to his father or what his father would say to him when he got there.

But what Vincenzo saw when he entered his father's hospital room shook him to the core. His mother was in a chair beside his father's bed, holding his hand in hers, softly singing to him. Even though Vincenzo recognized the tune as the one that they used to sing together so very many years ago, his father was unresponsive. He knew that rather than singing to his father's ears, his mother was singing to his father's soul.

Vincenzo was beyond moved. Then he saw his mother's eyes gently glide across the room to rest her gaze upon him. What he then witnessed was his aging mother's love and forgiveness as she absorbed the sight of her son after so many years. This was a moment forever frozen in his mind. This was also the moment that he felt his brother's hug for the first time in all those years.

"I want to make up with Papa. I want to say I'm sorry to him for all the pain I caused for not calling or visiting him for so many years," Vincenzo sobbed to his brother, whose only response was a grave shaking of his head, and a defeated wave of his hand toward the bed. Softly, his brother replied, "Papa's in a coma. He'll never come out of it."

The tears returned to Vincenzo as he continued, "When I left my family over all those years ago, I took for granted the love that filled my home - Momma, Papa, and my little brother. It was only in that hospital room when I realized the treasure that I threw away so many years ago.

After losing Papa and not having the chance to make up and say good-bye,
I vowed that I would cherish whatever time I had left with Momma. For the rest
of her life, I would give her all the love in my heart. And I did...until the moment
we lost her."

13. A RAGING EXECUTRIX

About a year after her brother, Dean, had passed away, Trudy came in my office to
discuss finalizing the administration of his estate. A number of questions had
suddenly arisen. Among these questions, the strangest one was her question as to
what her liability would be if one of the estate assets suffered damage. When I
asked her what the damage was and whether there was insurance for it, she
replied, "Well, actually, the damage hasn't happened yet." This puzzled me and I
asked her to please explain what she meant by "damage that had not yet
occurred." In order to put her question in the proper context, some background to
this story will be helpful.

Trudy described how her late father had become a very wealthy businessman.
After he passed away, his will divided his substantial estate equally between Trudy
and her brother, Dean. The two had always been very close siblings. Trudy had a
good marriage with her husband, but the same could not be said of Dean, whose
marriage to his wife, Helene, was what Trudy described as a nightmare. Even as a
sister-in-law, Trudy had feelings of hatred toward Helene.

I could see Trudy's expression harden as she described Helene's disgusting
treatment of Dean. Helene cheated on him openly and often. When Dean had his
first heart attack, she left him alone to recover at home, and went out night after
night to various night clubs. It was Trudy who was there to look after her ailing
brother, while Helene was out somewhere, drinking and dancing.

Even when Helene was pregnant, her drinking continued, unabated. As a
consequence, her only son, Kevin, was born with a form of fetal alcohol syndrome

which Trudy didn't want to start describing. Unquestionably, this devastated Dean. Trudy blamed Helene for hurting both father and son. Trudy cared for her brother and nephew while Helene was busy satisfying her own indulgences. Liquor, marijuana, and, eventually cocaine, were more important to her than her own son, and certainly more important to her than Dean.

Therefore, it was no surprise to anyone when Dean divorced her. The divorce was pitched warfare. Dean spent a fortune on his lawyer, battling down every attempt that Helene made to reach into his pocket. He ended up with moderate success. Apparently, Helene drowned her sorrows with a boyfriend.

After the divorce, Dean made a new will; named Trudy as his executrix; and left his entire estate to his son, Kevin. Less than a year later, at the age of fifty-five, Dean passed away from a second heart attack. Trudy felt that his untimely death came from the stress, anxiety, and frustration that were bottled up inside her brother; and she blamed Helene for all of it.

As I said, when Dean passed away, he left his fifteen-year-old son as the sole heir to his substantial estate. Trudy's task as executrix was to look after the estate because Kevin was under age; but that did not change the fact that the entire estate was left to him. One of the assets in Dean's estate was a precious Aston Martin convertible, which had been one of the few possessions which Dean had treasured. Trudy's eyes were tearing as she described how this was one way that Kevin could eventually step into his late father's shoes as he drove that car. Meanwhile, until Kevin would be old enough to drive, this family heirloom was stored in a specialty garage under a soft cotton cover.

The most shocking part of Trudy's story now unfolds, which brings us back to Trudy's question about damage to estate assets.

Helene called her. Trudy could hardly believe her ears when Helene told her that young Kevin had died. Helene said that he passed away from an aneurism and that now she wanted everything that Kevin owned. She was his only surviving parent. Without the slightest hint of remorse or sorrow in her voice, Helene demanded that Trudy turn over to her, everything that belonged to Kevin. She wanted it all right away.

Trudy had known enough about law to realize that a fifteen-year-old was not capable of making a will. Unfortunately, and in this case, tragically, Helene was indeed the lawful heir to her son's estate, and would now take everything. This was the law where this family lived, and this is exactly what Trudy had suspected.

Trudy was enraged that by inheriting from Kevin, Helene would now inherit whatever Dean had; and that inheritance not only included half of Trudy's father's wealth, but also the Aston Martin. When Trudy screamed to me, "that disgusting woman will never put her hands on Dean's car," I had to "read the riot act" to Trudy then and there because Trudy was starting to describe what she seriously wanted to do to that Aston Martin before Helene could get her hands on the vehicle.

Trudy at least managed to avoid an even worse ending to her series of misfortunes. She listened to reason; her better judgment prevailed; and she never did damage to or destroy the vehicle. This, at least, saved her from the serious lawsuit that Helene would have undoubtedly brought against her and won!

14. MR. INDISPENSABLE

"Do you own any shares in public companies?" When I asked Byron this question, his answer was, "No, I don't, not anymore. I'm sick about it, and I'll tell you why." Byron then told his story.

Byron always felt that he knew what was best for the company. Whenever another employee's contrary opinion arose from somewhere to stand in his way, Byron knew how to get rid of it. He would shout it down. Byron's tools included arrogance, insult, confrontation, or an attack on the ego of anyone who challenged him. As a result, the entire direction and focus of the company were driven by Byron, and for this reason, he felt that he really was driving the company.

However, nothing is forever; and the day came when Byron's shouting, insults, and anger simply did not work. Not only did Byron's opponent fail to back down, but this opponent even attracted many others to his side, to his point of view. So, Byron pulled out the heaviest weapon in his arsenal: ultimatum. Either everyone pulls together the way Byron tells them to, or Byron will quit. Inside his head, the logic ran as follows: if he quit, the company would no longer have Byron's knowledge and expertise. The company was doomed for failure, and they all would quickly lose their jobs.

In fact, Byron did quit. He sold his stock. He waited for everyone in the industry to see failure in a company that lost its way without him. But to Byron's surprise, as the weeks and the months rolled by, he saw the company's stock price rise. He saw fresh company ads in national magazines and newspapers. He saw the company advertising on national television. He read the complimentary reviews in the business media. With this, came his first feelings of embarrassment. He avoided contact with everyone in the industry. Byron's story comes to an end with these words of wisdom. "I guess I wasn't as valuable as I thought I was."

15. HOW WOULD YOU FEEL?

Vivian and Gil were giving me instructions for their wills. There was no controversy until I asked them who would be the guardian for their two children, who were in their early teens. At that point, Vivian said, "Gil has no siblings, and my only sibling is Kevin. So let's appoint my brother and his wife, Marlene." Gil immediately retorted, "No damned way! I can't stand Kevin or Marlene, and they will never raise my kids!"

I was taken aback by this sudden outburst, and Vivian was shocked, and replied, "What's wrong with Kevin and Marlene? They're the closest relatives we have."

Gil looked at me, and explained.

After Vivian's father died, Vivian and Gil spent an evening at Kevin and Marlene's house, viewing the father's old home videos. Vivian had taken all of her father's old videotapes to an electronics store and had transferred all of her father's tapes, even the very old ones, to DVD format.

The DVD she had made started with the oldest videos. Gil found the videos interesting, as he saw his wife, Vivian, and his brother-in-law, Kevin, as teenagers. After about a half-hour of watching the DVD, the scene of a backyard barbeque party came on the screen. Gil remembered that it was at this party that he first met Vivian's family. He had only been dating Vivian for a month at that time. He saw himself with his hair long, and dressed in jeans.

Vivian's father must have had the camera on a tripod. Gil saw everyone captured as the video camera panned all over the back yard. Then, unexpectedly, their father must have left the camera unattended, but with the videotape running. The lens became stationary, its focus resting on Kevin and Marlene speaking to another couple. They were close to the camera, but seemed oblivious to it because, if they been aware that the tape was rolling, the following dialogue would have never been recorded:

Kevin (to his new wife, Marlene): "Oh, my God. I can't believe my sister would bring that loser to our party. I hope she gets rid of him soon."

Marlene to Kevin: "Why would she even go out with a street bum like that? He doesn't belong with us. He should go back where he came from."

Third Party (unidentified): "Yeah, what a loser; he won't last with her."

Kevin to Third Party: "My Sis is too good for him. She'll dump him."

At that point, shocked by what he now heard from the video, Gil fumed. He jumped up, slammed the DVD player off its table and without one word, ran out to his car.

This all occurred about two years before my meeting with Gil and Vivian. Gil had not uttered so much as one word to either Kevin or Marlene since that time.

"So?" asked Gil. "Would you take that from anyone? Would you consider people like that family?" His questions were evidently directed at me, but Vivian scolded him. "Get over it! That was over twenty years ago."

Gil looked back at his wife. "They were not friends then, and they're not friends now. The video shows how they really felt about me and probably still do. I don't want them near our kids." Then Gil looked at Vivian and asked, "How would you feel if someone said that about you?" Vivian replied, "I understand your pain."

At this point in the meeting, they agreed on other guardians to name in their wills. After they left the meeting with me, I wondered if the new guardians would serve the children any better than the ones that Gil rejected. That is a question that will go unanswered in my mind.

16. HOW FAR CAN A PERSON GO?

Randy called in on a radio talk show to tell his story. He began by describing what it felt like to have his telephone ring constantly and without relief, even past midnight. The only way he could stop the ringing was to disconnect his home telephone and to turn off his cell phone. As soon as he either plugged in his home telephone or turned on his cell phone, they would instantly ring…from someone…who wanted to buy his car.

Randy, who lived on the east coast, then explained what led up to this nightmare. He spoke of a vicious court battle with his brother, who lived on the west coast. As a result of the fight over their father's estate, Randy was awarded his father's British racing green Jaguar XKE which is a most sought-after sports car. Almost immediately after Randy's disgruntled brother lost the court battle, someone placed an advertisement in a west coast newspaper, advertising the Jaguar for sale for a price which was ridiculously low. The advertisement gave Randy's home telephone number, and his cell phone number, as well. Not only did this person create an avalanche of nuisance calls for Randy, but worse yet, if someone from the west coast called at ten o'clock in the evening, that call would find its way to Randy's phone on the east coast at one o'clock in the morning due to the three-hour time difference.

Randy had no choice but to change his home telephone number. Unfortunately, he could not change his cell phone number because he was a salesman and needed this established number for his business. Randy told us and our radio show listeners that these advertisements for a bargain-basement-priced Jaguar were continuous for over six weeks. Furthermore, after investigating with the newspaper, it was then discovered that the source of these malicious advertisements was his disgruntled brother who lived on the west coast.

Randy's last comment was that he was about to be back in litigation with his west coast brother and asked if we knew any lawyers on the west coast. Randy and his brother had "raced" after their father's "race car," and would probably continue that costly race for many years to come. Our guess is that neither of them would consider himself a winner.

17. THE MONEY HOARDER

When they seat you at a wedding reception, chances are that at you will meet at least one new person, someone you have never met before. I was at a wedding where I enjoyed not one, but two strokes of luck. First of all, Connie, a bank employee, shared my table. The second stroke of luck was that the music was quiet, and I could actually carry on a conversation with her. This is where I learned the story of Herman.

What initially inspired Connie's comments was a discussion about people at the buffet, filling their plates to the top, and behaving like hoarders. She said this reminded her of a person she knew, 95-year-old Herman, a hoarder of money. Herman lost his wife many years ago; and the only remaining member of his family was his son, Louie.

Herman appeared to be a lonely man, and this is probably why he was visiting Connie at the bank every week. He always waited until Connie was free from her work tasks to talk with him. Herman did not want to deal with anyone else in the bank. Aside from looking at his bank balance, he loved to spend time talking to Connie about his son Louie who was a talented chef. Louie was the "best employee in the restaurant." Louie was "going places." One day Louie would "make it big." Connie could not keep herself from smiling when she added that Louie was about to turn 70.

Herman was an eccentric man. Connie described that from time to time, the bank would put on a promotion, and lay out a table of goodies for customers. There would be coffee, cakes, and candies. Herman was always there, it seemed, to fill and refill his cup, eat as much cake as he could, and stuff handfuls of candy into his pockets.

Herman drove an old Chevrolet, and always seemed to find a parking space at the very front of the bank's lot, and not too far from the window of Connie's office. She laughed as she described the vehicle. Aside from the fact that it was never washed, it seemed like the car was aging faster than Herman.

Connie remembered a time when Herman's car had intact mirrors outside its front doors. First one mirror, and then the other, suffered some kind of damage, and both were repaired with duct tape. The doors and fenders of the car were badly dented and scratched. She smiled again, as she recalled how these scratches seemed to multiply, week by week. The latest problem with his car was the muffler. The last time Herman came to visit the bank, his muffler was in such disrepair that she could hear the car coming before she could see it. She laughed again as she said that this frugal man would probably come to the bank next time with only three wheels on his car.

Herman's bank balance was a bit under five million dollars, and Connie made it clear to Herman that he was getting hardly any interest on his money. It was in a daily interest savings account. He really should be putting at least a few million in some kind of higher interest investment, even government bonds, she would advise him. Herman, however, was worried about having money at his fingertips to cover anything that might happen to him in his old age. As well, he was a suspicious man; and for weeks he kept asking Connie the same questions about whether his money would be safe. She quoted Herman: "If I keep all of my five million in a regular bank account, I can take it all out right away, if I hear the bank is closing up."

He told her that the first nickel he ever made was still in that account.

She found it very strange that this elderly man had so much money, yet, from what she could see, lived a life of poverty. She found it even stranger when Herman's son Louie came to see her last week.

She thought that Louie was there because Herman had sent him for some reason. She hoped that it wasn't because Herman was sick or that he had passed away. But when Louie explained to Connie why he was at the bank, her surprise turned to shock. Louie's visit had nothing to do with his father, Herman, and nothing to do with Herman's money. Louie was there because he made the decision to open up his own booth at a local farmer's market and was at the bank to ask for a two thousand dollar loan!

What was Louie's comment to Connie about the loan? "I told Dad that I needed the money to reserve the space for the booth; and if I couldn't get the money right away, I would lose the space to someone else. But he refused to give me any money or even to lend me the money, because he said he needed it if an emergency arose. He told me that he's saving all his money for me, and that I'll be a rich man one day. He also told me that now is not the time for me to get any of his money.

He said that he will only give it to me…after he dies."

After relating her story, Connie shook her head and said, "I will NEVER do that to my kids!"

18. GETTING REALLY, REALLY OLD

I was talking to a man about getting older and about how fast time flies which led him to share this joke with me:

There is a small village in Europe, which is reputed to be home to some of the world's oldest people. Peter, who hears about the extreme ages of the inhabitants, is so intrigued that he decides to fly to Europe to visit this village.

As he tours the village, he comes by a large pool where a woman is swimming at a racer's pace in an Olympic-sized pool. After watching her for several laps, he then sees her climbing up to a very high diving board and she does a perfect dive. She repeats this perfect dive two more times, then sits by the edge of the pool, and removes her bathing cap. Her hair is all gray, and, upon closer look, Peter realizes that she is very old.

Peter approaches her and says, "I am amazed at your stamina. I was very impressed with your swimming and diving. May I ask you how old you are?" She tells him she is 196 years old. Astounded, Peter asks her what her secret is. "I don't drink or smoke. I eat carrots and broccoli for breakfast, and blueberries with cottage cheese for lunch. Before I go to bed I eat a whole onion and a whole garlic clove, raw, from our local store." Peter thanks her, shaking his head in almost disbelief.

As he continues his walk into the village, he comes to a track where there are several runners about to compete. There is an elderly man in the far lane. A starter gun goes off and the runners sprint. Peter sees this man take an immediate lead on the other runners. As they run around the oval track, it is clear that the elderly man will not be overtaken. Coming around to the final stretch, he suddenly puts on a burst of speed, as if to show off. He finishes a full thirty seconds ahead of the second-place runner.

But, that is not the end of it. As the other runners head off, this elderly man goes back to the starting line to face a fresh set of competitors in a second race. Once again, he wins; and, for a second time, he finishes far ahead of the second-place runner.

Peter, hardly believing what he has just seen, goes up to this aged runner. "In my whole life, I have never seen running like what I just saw. If I may say, I have never imagined any senior citizen running like that. How old are you?" The man replies that he will be turning 200 the next week. Peter, now shocked, exclaims, "I must know your secret!" The elderly man says, "Lots of water, lots of whole grains, lots of vegetables, and a raw onion and a raw clove of garlic from our local store, before going to bed."

Peter has seen enough. He asks the elderly man where in the village this local store is located, and then he runs as fast as he can to this store, to buy the garlic and onions. Outside the store he sees a very, very old man sitting on a bench, under the store's awning. He looks twice the age of both the elderly swimmer and the aged runner he had just met. All around him are chicken bones, a littering of donut crumbs, fallen French fries, and greasy fried chicken boxes. He holds a vodka bottle in one hand, three-quarters empty. In his other hand, he holds a lit cigarette.

Peter pauses before going into the store, as fried foods, cigarettes, and vodka don't seem to fit into the picture of health and longevity that had been forming in his mind. "May I ask you, sir, what is your secret? What do you eat?" Peter needs to know the secret of this very old man.

"For breakfast, I smoke my first pack of the day. I then have donuts with cream cheese and wash them down with a beer or two. For lunch, I smoke another pack, have three or four boxes of fried foods, and wash them down with another beer or two. For dinner, I smoke another pack, and have a bag of chips, donuts, and lots of bacon. I wash them down with this vodka, and that is good enough for me."

"What about broccoli, fruit, and whole grains?" I asked. The elderly man replied, "Yuck! I can't stand them, and I never put them in my mouth."

"And don't you eat the local garlic and the onion from this store before you go to bed?"

"Never touch the stuff," says the man on the bench. "And this fast food, alcohol, and tobacco works for you?" asks Peter. "Sure does!" replies the man on the bench. Now, Peter wonders if the secret of longevity of this village is more mysterious than he had first thought.

"One final question," asks Peter of this ancient-looking man. "Just how old are you anyway?" Smiling, the man on the bench replies, "Next week I'll be 28!"

19. DEVALUING MOM'S LIFE

On a radio show about elder abuse, a woman called in to talk about how vulnerable her mother had been. She spoke about her brother, who moved in with Mom after he had separated from his wife. His wife had taken over the home that they had lived in, leaving him with no place to go. All of his money went to child support. For as long as our caller had known her brother as an adult, he was continually in debt.

Since Mom was getting around with a walker and was no longer driving, it seemed like a good idea at the time for Brother to move in with Mom. He could help her with shopping, cleaning, and other chores, and, even more importantly, he had a car. Our caller lived about four hundred miles away from Mom, whereas, Brother lived in the same city.

However, Brother moving in had turned out to be a big mistake. About three weeks after Brother moved in, Mom began to complain in tears to our caller about him. She could no longer get a good night's sleep; and, her blood pressure had risen to dangerous levels, along with her sugar levels, as she was diabetic.

Our caller explained that Mom had always kept her home neat, clean, and orderly. She hated clutter. She was a non-smoker. Furthermore, our caller emphasized how Mom said that she could not understand how her son could be in such a financial bind, since she and her late husband had always been savers, their home mortgage-free for many years.

Our caller attempted to describe Brother the way Mom described him. He was filthy and a heavy smoker who carried on his dirty habit in Mom's home. He was a hoarder. Mom's home was being overrun by junk, such as broken appliances which Brother intended to repair and sell. Greasy tools were staining the carpet and the kitchen floor. A wrecked car sat in the front yard, its windows broken, and a door hanging at an odd angle off its hinges. For the last couple of years, Mom had been using a ramp to her front door, to avoid her having to climb the stairs. This was especially important because now she was using a walker whenever she left the house.

When our caller recently went to visit Mom, she was shocked to see a pair of wooden oars beside the ramp, the ends of which extended into the ramp itself. In the daytime, these were serious obstacles for Mom, and at night, they would be an unseen hazard for her. Our caller immediately threw the oars onto a junk pile at the far end of the yard, a place, she pointed out, where Mom used to have a beautiful garden.

There was more for our caller to do inside the house, as it seemed to be laid out as an obstacle course. She was quickly exhausted, attempting to clear pathways inside the clutter where Mom might be able to walk. It was surprising to our caller that Mom had so far managed to avoid falling and breaking a leg or a hip. The refrigerator reeked from rotten, spoiled food. When our caller looked in the pantry, she saw more hazards, as some food cans were bloated and she could not find any "best-before" date markings which were current.

From the very beginning, Brother had ignored Mom's constant requests to clean up the place, to get rid of the junked car, to stop smoking in the house, and to clean up after himself. Worse yet, he called her a nag and kept telling her to get off his back. This, Mom told our caller, was Brother's way of thanking her for supporting him by paying his bills and by giving him as much money as he needed. And he seemed to need more and more as time progressed.

Our caller asked Mom why she didn't throw Brother out of the house, and Mom replied that he was her son, and she just couldn't turn a child of hers out into the street. With that, our caller said that what Brother wanted was not what she was giving him. She told Mom that what Brother really wanted was for Mom to get badly injured, or sick, and die so that he would get his share of her estate right away.

With that, our caller found two suitcases, packed whatever she could find of Mom's things, told Mom that they would work out all the details later, and took Mom to her own home to live. She wanted, without one more word, to get Mom away from the hazardous environment that Brother had created from Mom's beautiful home.

Our caller finished her story by saying, "My brother valued Mom more dead than alive."

20. I FOUGHT BACK

On a television call-in show, I received a call from Mary, who wanted to send a message to other seniors who might be in the same position as she had been. She was not a bit fearful if the guilty party happened to be listening to the show on that day. She told me how she fought back in her own way against financial elder abuse. This is her story.

She was a widow with two adult children. One child was her son who lived in his own home with his wife and children. He was a good son. Her other child was her daughter, who was single and who had been living with Mary for a number of years. Her daughter routinely did the shopping and various household chores. As well, she often, but not always, drove Mary to her medical appointments. Generally speaking, Mary's daughter performed the usual tasks that one might expect from a child who lived with a mother. However, it bothered Mary when her daughter referred to herself as a care-giver, because Mary referred to herself as an independent, 85-year-old woman. "She helped me out, but she certainly wasn't my care-giver."

Mary was generous to her daughter, and appreciative of her ongoing help. But an event which changed Mary's attitude toward her daughter occurred one morning, when her daughter wanted to "have a talk."

This "talk" consisted of complaints by Mary's daughter, that she was not being adequately compensated for what she was doing for Mary. The cash that she was getting from Mary was not enough. Mary's daughter wanted Mary's house to be given to her, mortgage-free, either now or after Mary died.

Offended by this, Mary told her daughter that there were two children in the family, not one, and that she had made a will leaving everything she had equally between her daughter and her son. Mary went on to point out that her son was good to her, as well, and that when it came to doing things for her, he was doing his fair share. Mary also reminded her daughter that she was living rent-free with Mary, while her son was paying his own way.

This infuriated Mary's daughter, and she threatened Mary, using language which more or less sounded this way: "If I don't get this house, then you can forget about any more help from me. If you fall, I won't even pick you up; and if you are weak in bed, you can lie in your own filth, and you better find someone to help you because I won't."

This "talk" frightened Mary. In order to keep peace in her home, she agreed to go to a lawyer and make a will leaving the house to her daughter. However, it was only when Mary handed over her signed will to her daughter that this stressful situation came to an end.

But Mary's story does not end here. You see, the way Mary fought back was to take the law into her own hands. During a week when her daughter was out of town, Mary arranged for a lawyer to come to her house to make a new will, revoking the one in her daughter's hands. The new will left Mary's entire estate to her son, cutting her daughter out. Mary intended to keep this second will secret from her daughter for the rest of her life. Mary concluded her call in a victorious tone, when she said, "I pacified my bullying daughter for the rest of my life with the fake will which had left my home to her, before I revoked the fake. My real will is leaving everything I own to my son, which is going to punish my daughter long after I am gone."

21. WHAT SHE GAVE UP TO SAVE TAX

Molly's story came to me from Pam, who attended a seminar on elder abuse. Pam wanted to share Molly's story with me so that I could write about it, as a wake-up call to seniors.

Pam was in the express-pay line in a supermarket. Ahead of her stood Molly, an elderly woman who used a walker. When it came time for Molly to pay for her few items, she rummaged in her purse for money which just wasn't there. The minutes ticked by as Molly emptied the contents of her purse onto the cashier's counter. Pam could see that the only items which had to be paid for were a loaf of bread, a bunch of celery, a small bag of carrots, and a package of cheese. There were impatient grumblings from behind, probably from those in the third, fourth, or fifth positions in the line. Pam felt very sorry for this elderly woman, who was evidently embarrassed. Pam could see Molly's hands shaking and detected panic in this poor woman.

Immediately, Pam offered to pay the $5.85 showing on the cashier's display. Molly, now flustered, managed to say that she was a proud woman, and that she would just forget about buying anything. But Pam insisted upon paying, quickly providing a ten-dollar bill to the cashier. Molly was moved, and asked if she could meet Pam outside the store after Pam finished paying for her food. She wanted Pam's address so she could mail the money to repay her. Pam insisted that she didn't want the money back, but Molly was waiting for Pam by the exit door to the supermarket.

Molly already had a pen and paper in hand as she was waiting for Pam, and again asked for her address. They began to talk, and the first thing that Molly told Pam was that she would send the money to Pam at the beginning of the next month, when her allowance from her children came in. Molly explained that right now, her children had all of her money because in a weak moment, she had given it all to them, and now she was living in fear. When Pam asked how this predicament came about, Molly told her the following story.

About two years earlier, her children convinced her that in order to save taxes at her death, Molly should sell her home and transfer everything she owned to them, so that when she died there would be nothing in her name. Her children would put her on a monthly allowance until she died. Her children said that this monthly allowance should be enough to cover her monthly living expenses. Last month, Molly had to beg her daughter for some extra money, and her daughter gave it to her, but along with this money, came a scolding. Molly's daughter yelled at her and gave her a harsh talking to, telling Molly that she was wasting money. So, that is why there would be no money for Pam, or for anyone else, until the beginning of the next month. Molly said that she was afraid to ask her children for more money because she did not want to be belittled again by them.

Pam remembered the last words she heard from Molly that day: "This is what happens to a trusting mother like me. This was all my money. I gave control of it to my children, and now I am terrified to ask for any of it back."

22. SHOES IN THE HALL OF LES' HOME

I hear many people say that they find life passing them by so quickly - too quickly, in fact. They often cast their minds back to events which occurred many years ago, and hold onto these memories for comfort. I strongly empathize with everyone who feels this way. More pointedly, the following comments, about shoes in the hall of my home, relate to the way I measure time, and how fast it slips away.

"When my first daughter was still crawling on her hands and knees, there were no shoes in the hall of my home. But once she started walking, there were always one or two pairs of tiny pastel-colored shoes there, the kind that had Velcro straps. Two pairs became three, then four, and by the time my second daughter began to walk, you had to step carefully when you came in the front door so as not to trip on one of these shoes. Then came the birthday parties, the laughter, the noise, and a front carpet full of these little shoes from my daughters' little friends.

Somehow, time passed by, and the little Velcro shoes were mixed with, and then were replaced by, lace running shoes. Then, more time passed by, and the running shoes became leather, dressier shoes. Boys would start coming over, and their shoes were now mixed with the girls' shoes. Time kept passing so the size of the shoes kept getting bigger, therefore, taking up more space. As well, the noise level in the house was increasing, as the teenager parties were filling our home with music and with laughter.

Before you realized it, the girls' shoes had little heels, then higher heels, and the boys' shoes became young men's dress shoes.

Suddenly, one daughter moved out, and on with her life, then the other. With both of my girls living on their own, the piles of shoes in the hall have gone. Their parties and their music have gone. My house is now quiet. My wife and I are now empty-nesters. How did all of this happen so fast?

Now, whenever I see shoes in the hall of my home, the sight makes me so happy because when I see those shoes, it means that one or both of my daughters have come home to pay my wife and me a visit.

I just can't believe how fast the time has flown. You turn your head and it's gone."

23. UN-WILL-ING

A lawyer called us, after reading about our firm in a magazine article. He said that he had a great story for our next book. What he wished to share with us was his experience with the most unusual estate in all his experiences. The lawyer referred to the deceased as "Clement," who had made a home-made will, which named this lawyer as executor. One of the nurses in the nursing home in which Clement had passed away, called the lawyer because the lawyer's name was in the will, and the lawyer's phone number was attached to it.

The lawyer was astounded after reading Clement's will. It was unlike anything the lawyer had ever seen. The will did not leave anything to anyone. It only described who was not getting anything. The will also gave the reasons why each of the parties named in it got nothing. The lawyer described this document as a "negative will."

The lawyer had done some research, and, from all the information that he had gathered, this was the background. Clement died as a widower, with no children, and all of his siblings had passed away before he did. The lawyer also found that Clement's siblings had no children.

However, Clement did have three brothers-in-law who were alive.

The will referred to these brothers-in-law, not as beneficiaries, but as adversaries. In other words, none of them got anything. The lawyer said, "The will is short, I want to read it to you, but you better sit down."

"Brother-in-law Merlin, you get nothing because you are an idiot, and you have cost me thousands of dollars with your bad investment advice. You may think you're a licensed, financial advisor, but I will repeat, you are an idiot!"

"Brother-in-law Troy, you get nothing, because you are a home-wrecker. I knew all along about your affair with my wife."

"Brother-in-law Cecil, you get nothing because you are the crooked, good-for-nothing, used car salesman who sold me a 1965 Plymouth. The damned car was so damaged by flood and mold that I couldn't sit it the car for more than five minutes without wanting to throw up. You even refused to give my money back. Great brother-in-law you are!"

Sonya, his former care-giver also got nothing. In Clement's words, "Sonya, I know you stole most of my underwear and pajamas and took them home to give to your husband."

His friends Boris, Hilda, and Murray got nothing either. Again in Clement's words, "Boris, you never once knew when I had my birthday. You either called me one month too early or one month too late. Hilda, thanks for telling my wife about my affair with my secretary. This really helped my marriage. Murray, every conversation we ever had was about one thing: you, not me. Some friends you all were. I hope you all enjoy spending your own money, not mine!"

The lawyer had trouble with this reading because he continually interrupted his narrative with the laughter he could not hold back. But the lawyer sobered up at the end of our discussion when he realized the headache that now faced him, trying to figure out who the real heirs were, now that what appeared to be a will, really left him as executor, to administer a wild goose chase. His last comment was, "It's really as if there was no will, and now I need to find out if there is anyone who was related to this man. If I ever find him or her, I can only imagine the smile on his or her face when that person gets three million dollars from a man he or she has probably never met!"

24. THE KNIFE IN DAD'S HEART

It's not as if Kayla and her three brothers had always gotten along with each other; but when Dad's health started to go downhill, all four siblings agreed amongst themselves that in Dad's presence, they would never argue and would never speak of sickness or death. All they agreed to speak of in his presence was the upbeat, the comical, only those special warm subjects that make people happy.

Their agreement worked well and did bring cheer to Dad, which they could tell by his constant smile whenever they were together with him. Even when he had to be hospitalized, that smile of his seemed to push away the reality of his rapidly-deteriorating health.

The doctor had called Kayla in the morning. His news was not good, and he had asked Kayla to call her brothers together so that the four of them could pay their final respects to their father at the hospital.

Dad's smile greeted them as they entered the room. It was as if the fact he was dying was pushed away, once again. The discussion was again upbeat, and pictures, report cards, comments on the successes of grandchildren, and a bowling trophy kept that smile on Dad's face. But the tone in the room turned very dark when Kayla suddenly began a barrage of questions. "Dad, what about the house? You left me the house in your will, right? Should I call a lawyer to come here right now to make sure it's in your will? Am I going to be able to still live there when you die? You know I deserve the house more than they do! And, where's the will, Dad?"

As Dad heard these words, his eyes filled with tears, and that smile left his face, never to return. Her words made her brothers furious with her. But, with those words now out of her mouth, they could never be taken back.

It's as if Dad died twice. Once, when he heard Kayla's selfish outburst, and the second time, the next morning, when the doctor pronounced Dad dead.

25. LEAVING THE 1970'S

One of the topics in an article which quoted us, spoke of the will as a living and breathing document, to be kept up-to-date in order to reflect changing circumstances. A lawyer who practiced in another jurisdiction, having read the article, called to tell us that the article was dead-on correct. The lawyer represented an estate where the deceased did not believe in keeping his will updated. As a result, the estate was beset by innumerable problems. In the words of that lawyer, "What a mess that man left for his family!"

He referred to the deceased as "Mr. Smith," who had his last will made in 1973. Although, at first glance, the wording of the will seemed reasonable, in fact, it was sadly outdated.

Forty years after making his will, Smith passed away. The year was 2003. His estate went to probate on his 1973 will. The lawyer first emphasized that Smith never updated his will to accommodate changes which occurred in his own life, and in the world at large. He then walked us through the problems that were interwoven into the administration of this ill-constructed estate:

The will appointed Smith's wife as sole executrix, and, if she died before him, then Smith's brother, Ned, would be the executor. Both Smith's wife and brother Ned died years before Smith did.

Problem #1: With wife and brother both gone, there was no executor left to look after Smith's estate.

Smith's will initially left his entire estate to his wife; but if she died before him, Smith's will distributed various household items to Kelly and Harrison, his two sons, which were the only children he had in 1973. Smith's will made reference to his Philco television set; a Polaroid instant camera; a cassette tape player; a Dual turntable and an 80 watt hi-fi set; a Corvus hand-held calculator; a collection of eight-track cassettes; and an Akai reel-to-reel tape recorder. According to Smith's will, in order to decide which of his sons would get each particular item, his sons, Kelly and Harrison, would have to flip a coin in front of their uncle Ned.

Problem #2: Not one of these items survived the passage of time, and Ned died years ago.

Smith left his son, Kelly, his Gremlin, which was one of the cars he owned when he made his will. The will provided that if at the time of his death, he didn't own the Gremlin, then Kelly would get any other American Motors car owned by Smith at the time of his death. Smith's will left his other car, his Valiant, to his son, Harrison. The will provided that if at the time of his death, Smith didn't own the Valiant, then Harrison would get any other car owned by Smith at the time of his death, as long as that car was not manufactured by American Motors.

Problem #3: When Smith died in the year 2003, he didn't own either the Gremlin or the Valiant. Furthermore, American Motors had long since ceased to carry on its business under this name. The wording of Smith's will meant Kelly did not inherit any car, because in order for Kelly to inherit a car, Smith would have to own either the Gremlin, or another American Motors product, when he died. As it turned out, Smith did own two cars when he died, but they were a Ford Mustang and a Toyota Camry. The strange result of the wording of Smith's will now meant that Harrison was entitled to both the Mustang and the Camry. In the words of the lawyer, "Two for Harrison, zero for Kelly."

Smith's will also divided the stocks he owned in 1973 between Kelly and Harrison. The will made reference to the market price of the shares, which were of approximate equal value.

Problem 4: Kelly inherited shares in a now-defunct and worthless clothing company. However, Harrison inherited IBM shares, which had escalated vastly in value since 1973.
The lawyer commented, "It was another shutout for Kelly because of Smith's outdated will."

Smith's will left Kelly his primary residence on Whitecliffe Road. If Smith didn't own that property when he died, his will said that Kelly would get any other primary residence that Smith owned and lived in at the time of his death.

On the other hand, Smith's will left his winter beachfront vacation home in Florida to his son, Harrison.

Problem 5: At the time of his death, Smith did not own the property on Whitecliffe Road. Whitecliffe was never replaced. However, Smith kept the Florida winter home. There was no certainty as to whether, at the time of Smith's death, this could be interpreted as Smith's primary residence. The lawyer needed more information in order to deal with this matter. For the moment, the way the estate appeared to the lawyer, because Smith's will specifically left Harrison the Florida beachfront property, he seemed to have won out again. Kelly may well still receive no property, unless somehow the Florida property could be interpreted as a replacement property for the original primary residence. Could this be a future court battle? Yes.

Smith's will left the rest of what he owned equally between Kelly and Harrison. The two brothers had the privilege of getting a baby sister in 1976 and another baby sister in 1978. One of the sisters was supported by and lived with Dad until he died; and the other of the two girls was disabled and relied upon Dad's financial help to survive.

Problem 6: What were the two girls entitled to from their father's estate? Is there a possible court battle between the two sisters and the two brothers?

Final comment of the lawyer who contacted us: "What a mess!"

26. TRYING TO MAKE AN IMPRESSION

We heard this joke from a lawyer.

Hector had never been an "A" student in law school, but when it came to being aggressive, it was hard to find a match for him. His aggressiveness led him to win over Isabel, a beautiful young woman, who was most impressed with the fact that Hector was opening up his law practice right after getting his admission to the bar.

So impressed was Isabel that she wanted to be there on the first day that Hector opened his law office. She sat in his brand new waiting room, where there were four chairs, and a receptionist desk. Hector didn't have a receptionist yet, so he sat at the new receptionist desk that had just been installed.

To Hector's surprise, just as he and Isabel were sitting in the reception area talking to one another, in walked a young man. "Aha! Another client!" bragged Hector. Gorgeous Isabel was impressed. A beautiful woman has a lot of choices, and this made her proud of choosing a winner.

Hector motioned to the young man, to sit with them. "I'll call you into my private office in a moment; but just wait; I have two important calls I must make to a couple of other lawyers."

And with that, Hector grabbed the phone, punched in some numbers, and after waiting a moment, exclaimed, "I represent the Dylan Franks Estate. You know that he has sold over fifty million records and your client has breached copyright." For the next several minutes, the young man and Isabel heard Hector rifle off the legal steps his client would take if the problem was not resolved. And, as proud as she had been, Isabel was beaming now, especially with Hector's final exclamation into his phone, "You don't know who you are dealing with. I mean business!"

After that call, Hector motioned with his hand to Isabel and the young man, "I have to make just one more call." Again, punching in some numbers, and waiting for a moment, Hector exclaimed into the phone, "We are going to court on that will unless you do better than that twenty-five million dollar offer on the table. You better get back to me before tomorrow night! And I mean tomorrow night, at the latest!"

Isabel could hardly contain herself. And now to the young man who had patiently waited with Isabel. "How can I help you, sir? What is your legal problem?" asked Hector, who could not help taking in Isabel's broad smile. "Oh, I am not here for legal help. I work for the phone company and I am here, sir, to set up your phone lines!"

27. THE FIRST WIFE

A funeral director we met thought we would appreciate this joke.

At the gravesite, Fannie could not hold back her grief, while hugging the headstone so closely that she covered every word written on it. Her tears would not stop. Over and over she cried, "Why did you have to die? Why did you die?!! Why did you have to die so soon?"

An old acquaintance of Fannie's happened to have been in the same cemetery, attending a funeral, and heard Fannie crying. The friend came over to console her. Putting her arms around Fannie, her friend said, "I'm so sorry for your loss. I see your tears. You must have loved your husband so much. I didn't know he passed away."

"My husband? That miserable S.O.B. is still alive. This grave belongs to his first wife!"

28. I LOVE YOU ALL

We were at a lunch break at a legal convention, sitting with a number of other lawyers. A female lawyer recognized us as the authors of The Family Fight, Planning to Avoid It, and said that she had another story to share with our readers.

She then told of her experience with her client, Marvin, who had met her to discuss his instructions for his will. She described Marvin as a man of surprises. He did not have a commanding voice, yet this gentleman immediately took control of the appointment, setting out how he wanted to distribute his considerable wealth.

Sophie, his wife of forty years, would get half the estate, Ingrid would get one-quarter, and, Martine would get one-quarter. He chose his bank to look after his estate as its executor. The lawyer then asked him what he wanted to provide for, in the event that something unexpected were to occur. In other words, she needed to know Marvin's intentions, if one of these beneficiaries passed away before he did.

When the lawyer asked who would inherit in place of the girls if one of them predeceased him, Marvin required a bit of an explanation.

"What if Martine predeceased you? Would Sophie inherit what Martine was to get?" He thought about it, and then decided that he wanted her share divided equally between Sophie and Ingrid. Then the lawyer asked what would happen if his daughter, Ingrid, predeceased him. "Daughter?" Marvin laughed. "Ingrid's my girlfriend!" "What about Martine?" "She's also my girlfriend!" "Does your wife Sophie know of this?" Marvin replied, "None of these three women know of the other two. Too bad I won't be able to see the look on each of their faces after I am gone!"

The lawyer finished her story by describing what happened when she and her secretary witnessed the will. In fact, right up until the will was witnessed, only the lawyer and Marvin himself knew this secret.

The lawyer went on to tell us, "After Marvin left the office, I asked my secretary if she knew who Martine and Ingrid were. 'They must be his daughters?' replied my secretary. I responded, 'No, they're both his girlfriends, and, none of the women in his will know of the other two!'"

Her secretary howled with laughter. The lawyer left us with the comment that both she and her secretary hoped that they would be around to handle Marvin's estate because they wanted to also write a book. She and her secretary felt like they had only witnessed one chapter of a very juicy book. We agree and think it has potential to be a best-seller in this field!

29. FROM THE MOUTH OF BABES

A few weeks after Mom's funeral, Ken and his sister, Tess, met a real estate agent to sell Mom's home. It had always been a warm place; and Tess's seven-year-old daughter, Madison, had spent a good part of her early years at Grandma's house. It was Grandma, while she was still in good health, who had looked after Madison while Tess was working.

The agent listed the home, but selling it was not so easy. After a month or so had passed, the agent suggested lowering the price. Still there were no takers.

Over the next several months, the price was lowered again, and, yet again. Finally, the agent called. There was a buyer! They all wanted to be at Grandma's when the buyer came. The agent cautioned them that it was not the usual thing to do, but they were insistent. Ken wanted to speak of the warmth of the place. Tess wanted to be there because she didn't want Ken to be alone. And, Madison had to come because there was no one to babysit for her.

The meeting with the buyer took place after the supper hour. It went well, but the agent wanted to get down to paperwork. He wasn't pleased to have first Ken, then Tess, speak of all their happy years in the place. This wasn't good for business. But there was no way the agent could signal to them to just shut up and let the buyer's good mood lead to a signature on a page.

Meanwhile, little Madison heard her uncle say such nice things about Grandma's place; and then she heard Mom follow up with more nice comments. She felt left out. Yet she was the one who had spent more time with Grandma than either of them. So, she just had to contribute something.

The little girl spoke up, and with smiles, Ken, Tess, the agent, and the buyer all stopped talking so the cute little one could put in her two cents' worth.

"Grandma's place was really good, especially when it rained really hard, because Grandma and I would play splash and I would put my boots on when all the water came into the basement!"

The buyer promptly left.

30. HE CAN SEE FOREVER

Sometimes the strangest things bring happiness. After a client gave me his instructions to make a will, he asked if I wished to see a picture that made him really happy. I expected to see a photograph of one of his grandchildren, or of his cottage, or perhaps a sailboat. But, all I could see in the picture was grass and trees on a hillside. "This is my own cemetery plot," he said, beaming. "I beat my brother to it. He always got what he wanted but not this time. It's on a hill. It overlooks the main street of my town. I will be able to hear the birds in the trees that overlook my plot. I am going to find eternal peace there."

I was at a loss for words at this point. But, what really amounted to a punch line to this story were his next words, "By the way, can you put a clause in my will that I have to be buried wearing my glasses? I want to make sure I enjoy this view forever!"

31. THE BROKEN MAN

Joe had come to make a new will. I could not help but notice that he was wearing a baseball cap upon which the letters "WWII VET" were written. When Joe saw me staring at his cap, he mentioned that he had been a sergeant in the Second World War. He described himself as an old man, but he was proud to have served his country. He said that he was tough with the men under him, but fair. He had a deep and rough voice, and his handshake was powerful and strong. His posture, at least at the beginning of our meeting, spoke military to me.

Joe had come to give instructions about his will, but also said that he had a lot on his mind that he had to unload. I told him that he was free to tell me whatever he wished to tell.

Joe started then by speaking of his first wife, Clara, and baby Clifford, both of whom he had to leave back home when he was called to serve in the Second World War. When Joe came back from the war, he found young Clifford tightly bonded to Clara. It took a lot of patience and effort for Joe to try to be the father and husband that he had imagined he would be, during his fighting years. But this was not to be. Clara unexpectedly died while Clifford was still a little boy.

Joe tried to be both mother and father to Clifford. This was as tough as anything he had ever undertaken. He had a lot of work to do to develop the type of bond that Clifford must have had with his mother. This uphill battle continued for about four years after he lost Clara, when Maureen entered his life. Joe quickly fell in love with her, but Clifford seemed cold and distant. This was a problem that neither Joe nor Maureen could solve.

Several more years passed, and no matter what he said or did, Joe could not bridge the emotional distance between himself and Clifford. Then, shortly after Clifford had turned fifteen, father and son finally had a heart-to-heart talk. This is when Clifford told Joe that what he did to Mom was unforgiveable. Confused, Joe asked his son what he was talking about. Clifford said that it was cruel for Joe to find another woman so soon after Clara was gone. Joe was shocked. There were no words he could find to explain to Clifford that he loved Clara, and would never do anything to offend her, or her memory. He said that he was a soldier, and Clara knew that he might never return. Between them, they had made a pact that either of them could move on with their lives if one of them were to die young.

But none of this made a dent on Clifford's hard shield of anger. He retreated even further from his father. Their household was one of contrasts. Warmth, love, and bonding between Joe and Maureen on the one hand, as opposed to icy silence between Clifford and his father on the other. As for Maureen, all Joe could say was that Clifford hated Maureen, and she tolerated Clifford. This stalemate lasted about three years, when Clifford announced that he was leaving permanently and never wanted to see or hear from them again. This may not have been surprising to Joe, but that didn't make it any less painful.

At this point in Joe's narrative, Joe began to clear his throat, and I began to see a change in his composure. He was silent for a couple of moments and then continued with what he had to say.

More than two decades passed during which Joe didn't know where his son was, or even if he was alive. One evening while he was at home with Maureen, the telephone rang. It was Clifford. This was the most uplifting moment Joe could remember ever since the day he met Maureen. Clifford had married, and had a son. There appeared to be a softening of the situation that had grated on Joe over all these years. Clifford wanted to meet. He said he had a lot to talk about.

Clifford came over to the house. He spoke of the years that had passed, and of the various jobs he had held. He also spoke of the possibility of moving closer to Joe and Maureen. With Joe's financial assistance, Clifford might be able to buy a home in the same city as Joe, and re-connect with them. Joe did not have enough comfort with Clifford to buy a home for him, but he did offer to pay rent for Clifford and his family for a year, if Clifford would move to his city. Father and son shook hands on that; Clifford made the move; and during that year, they met every second weekend. Joe did not say that these meetings were warm, but at least there was, from Joe's point of view, hope. Clifford had upheld his end of the bargain, and Joe did not let Clifford down. He not only paid the rent, but also, from that point onward, continued to give Clifford extra money to help him make ends meet.

However, Joe seemed to have a pattern to his life. Just when it looked like he had climbed over an obstacle, another one seemed to arise from nowhere. Consistent with this pattern, the next event in Joe's life was his loss of Maureen, which was a devastating loss.

Then Joe spoke of the recent series of events that had led to his appointment with me. About two weeks before our appointment, Clifford had asked for $250,000 to help with the start-up of a new business. But this time, Joe had to refuse. Joe did not have the money, and there was no way that Joe would mortgage his home for a business that could easily fail. Joe's refusal was met with Clifford's silence.

The next day, Joe called Clifford, but only got his voicemail. Clifford did not call him back. A few days later, Joe called again, but still could not get beyond Clifford's voicemail. Finally, Joe went to Clifford's home and rang the bell, but no one answered.

This ongoing silence was finally broken a few days before my appointment with Joe. On a Monday morning, Joe had accidentally slipped on the floor in his house. While he was uninjured, his only pair of eyeglasses broke. Without them, he was lost. His sight was badly impaired without glasses, and he certainly could not drive a car. So, Joe called Clifford, to ask him if he could drive him to the optometrist. Voicemail again. Then Joe began to leave his message of desperation, in the hope that Clifford might quickly get back to him. Moments after Joe left the desperate message, Clifford did call back. At first, Joe was relieved, but his relief was short-lived. Joe began to show emotion as he attempted to repeat the conversation between himself and his son:

Joe: "I'm so relieved you called back so soon. I really need your help. You know, as well, I've called several times and left messages and I even went to your house. I guess you were away."

Clifford: "I wasn't away. I got all of your messages and when you rang the doorbell I knew it was you and none of us answered the door."

Joe: "Why? What's the problem?"

Clifford: "You're the problem. The only reason I answered this call is to tell you once and for all that I hate you. You're a cheap slimebag and I don't need you or your money anymore. You can fix your own eyes the way you fixed our family. You should have smashed your head instead of your glasses. I despise you, and always have. You can forget about ever seeing me again!"

After what Joe told me, it was no surprise that he instructed me to make out his will, cutting out Clifford, and leaving everything to a charity that looked after veterans of the Second World War.

However, my own surprise did not come from these instructions, but rather from the fact that they came from a man who had weathered, survived, and even rebounded from so much in his life that was tragic. "I've slept in freezing temperatures in muddy foxholes, saw dead bodies around me, and saw towns burned out and ravaged. I endured the loss of too many of my closest friends to a miserable war. And when it was all over, not once, but twice, the women I loved so much were taken from me."

Through all of these tragedies and others that Joe was now describing, I have no doubt that Joe must have shown a brave face. But recalling and repeating Clifford's scathing words to me pushed Joe's composure over a line that, without a doubt, Joe had not allowed himself to cross for many years.

Excusing himself, Joe turned away from me, his face to the window. Although now his back was to me, I could see his hands raised to cover his face. I respected his privacy and his silence, as a few moments passed. Then he turned around to face me again, wiped away tears from his eyes, stuffed a used tissue into his pocket, and looked at me, evidently embarrassed, and said, "Sir, I am so sorry that you have to see me like this. It has never happened to me before. Of everything I've gone through in my life, this has destroyed me and made me weak enough to break down. You're the only person in the world who has ever seen me cry."

32. THOUGHTS ABOUT LIFE AND MONEY FROM INSIDE OUR WORLD

(a) Tanya told me about the good news. Her father and her uncle had settled their differences after many years of fighting with one another. The two brothers were now well into their eighties. Their settlement not only resolved financial matters, but also managed to restore the peace between them. Tanya's comment was memorable: "I could never understand two brothers losing so many years out of a lifetime. It is not as if they had seven hundred more years to live."

(b) Isabel and her brother were debating over what to do with several hundred thousand dollars left to them from their late father's estate. Isabel put her case this way:
"Our disagreement was over numbers, which mean different things to different people. My brother wanted to keep the money invested inside the estate; but I felt the time to distribute it was right now, as we were already in our seventies. I haven't been well, and my brother was taking his health for granted. While my brother was speaking of stock and real estate prices, bond yields and interest rate returns, I told him he was ignoring the real numbers. I took him by surprise, because he could not imagine any way that an immediate distribution of the monies would get a better return than what he was telling me. Then he was really taken by surprise when I told him what the real numbers were. Cholesterol count, white blood cell count, blood pressure reading, and sugar level."

(c) Daisy was 80 years old and had lost her sight at the age of five. In the course of my discussion with her, she said that she had gone over seventy-five years without seeing what was around her. When I had asked her what she did remember seeing, she described beautiful brown horses which were kept on her parents' farm, and the greenness of the fields on a brilliantly sunny day. She also recalled very tall trees, and the veins which ran through the leaves that fell to the ground. All these images stayed in her mind. I had asked Daisy what was the one thing that she wished she could have seen over so many years. She immediately responded, "I wish I could have seen the face of the man I married and the face of my only child. Now, they are both gone, but I can only imagine how beautiful they were."

(d) Bradley was upset when he came to do his will. He felt that Evan, his only child, did not appreciate him. Evan's own son, a teenager, had just been enrolled in a private school, which Evan could not easily afford. So, Evan asked Bradley for money to pay for the private school. Bradley felt that this would be too much of a drain on his own finances, and he refused. That is when Evan threatened to cut off all relations with Bradley, saying that there would be no more visiting, no more calls, and that as far as Evan was concerned, Bradley could be alone for the rest of his life, and would never again see his grandson.

In response, Bradley reminded Evan that he had paid for his university education, his wedding, and had helped Evan with everything he had asked for. Evan responded, "Dad, stop living in the past. That's ancient history; let's talk about what I need now!"

At this point, Bradley looked at me, shook his head, and said, "What happened to the words 'Thanks, Dad?'"

(e) None of Kenny's friends seemed to understand why he was so upset when his 93-year-old father passed away. The common attitude among these friends seemed to be, "Sorry your father died, but you must realize he had lived a long life and it is a gift for anyone to get to that age." Kenny was with me to look after his father's estate. He told me that he was very upset with his cold and heartless friends who trivialized his elderly father's passing.

The way Kenny put it: "When I was a young child, my Dad was my hero. Whatever he said, I looked up to him for it. In my teens, he was a strict task master against whom I rebelled. Whatever he said, I seemed to do the opposite, and often to my own detriment. In my 30's, after Mom died, and after I met my wife and we had our child, Dad became my mentor. He was the grandfather; I was the dad; and I cherished his wise advice.

Before long, Dad had his 60th birthday, and, by then he had become my rock. For over 30 years from that point, we were very close; and every moment I spent with him was precious to me. So, you can see why I say that my friends just don't get that I am heartbroken. I don't care how old my Dad was. To me, he was not an old man. He was my very best friend in the world."

(f) Gaetan had called to ask if we had a book in our office which lists registered charities. He explained that he had no family to whom to leave an estate. When I

met with him, I saw a sad individual, who had a need to vent some deeply pent-up emotions. Gaetan explained that his whole life might have been different had he decided, years ago, to make a commitment to the girl he had gone out with during his early university years, and who had wanted to marry him.
But Gaetan had to see the world before making a final commitment; and he set out to travel on his own.

But on his return, Gaetan felt his first real pain when the girl he loved so much had begun to date other men. That pain only deepened when he learned that she had gotten married. He pulled out the picture of a very beautiful woman that he had kept in his wallet over so many years. "Why didn't I marry her? I only wish that I could be coming to you now, to leave all my hard-earned estate to my wife and children. I could have had a beautiful family and a happy life. I should have done the right thing when I had the chance. The older I get, the more pain I feel from the mistakes I made years ago."

His summary of his situation was this: "Regrets are magnified by time."

(g) Elise was very upset. She was one of four beneficiaries of her recently deceased grandfather's estate, and she was at our office for advice. Elise described how Grampa started life here with hardly more than the shirt on his back. Through a combination of hard work, foresight, good timing, and skill, he had accumulated a number of commercial buildings.

As a young teenager, Elise worked with Grampa, collecting and recording rent, cleaning up vacant premises, and performing innumerable other tasks. She made a point of telling me that under Grampa's will, her three cousins, Grampa's other grandchildren, were now her partners in the building business that Grampa left. Grampa always told Elise that he was going to leave the company which owned this portfolio of buildings to Elise and her three cousins. Grampa wanted his four grandchildren to work together as a family to continue to build the business in which he had invested his heart and soul. These buildings were the love of his life.

What brought Elise to our office was her disappointment with the conduct of her three cousins, now that Grampa was no longer alive. She met with them the week before to discuss some of the financial issues relating to the buildings. To her surprise, what they told her was this: They did not care that Grampa had built this business for them. They did not want the buildings, did not want to deal with tenant issues, the roof, the air conditioning, the lines on the parking lot, or anything else. They just wanted the money that the buildings were worth, and demanded that the company put everything up for sale.

In the words of her eldest cousin, "We just want the cash. We'll be worth a fortune once these buildings are sold; so, we don't want to work; we don't have to work; and we don't care if we have to sell the buildings at a discount in order to get the cash now! Grampa may have loved these buildings, but we don't!"

(h) Crystal's contribution to our seminar on the subject of inheritance took me by surprise. She smiled, shaking her head. "Inheritance is not all that it's cut out to be. Bank accounts? Stocks and bonds? Let me tell you what I got from my parents. From my mom, I got her high blood pressure and cholesterol. What my dad left me was his diabetes and glaucoma!"

33. IT SEEMS LIKE IT WAS ALL FOR NOTHING

Jayne's mood was dark and angry when she came to do her will. She gave me instructions to cut out both of her adult children. She did not need much coaxing to spill out her story; but just before she began, she said that her instructions were going to show that her children had driven multiple daggers into her heart.

She explained that her husband had separated from her about ten years ago. It was very bitter. It took her totally by surprise. The last thing she wanted was a marriage breakdown, especially since her life had been so good before the sudden change. She had raised both of her children with a loving heart. She was a stay-at-home mother, and devoted most of her time and attention to their wellbeing, their schooling, their after-school activities, and to all of their other needs. "I never left their side. When they were sick, I stayed up nights. I attended every parent-teacher's night. I helped them with all of their homework. Every night before they went to sleep, they got a kiss and a hug from me."

What surprised Jayne most of all was that, at the time of her separation from her husband, her relationship with her two children deteriorated to the point that they stopped talking to her altogether. They were blaming Jayne for making their dad leave them; and the children were taking his side. After that, her birthdays began to pass without cards, gifts, or even phone calls from either of the children. She tried to send gifts to her children and they were always returned. The children were never at any family functions or affairs of cousins or other relatives which Jayne attended. She felt that they wanted to avoid the possibility of seeing her. When she attempted to contact them, either they hung up the phone on her, or, if she left a message, the call was never returned.

She felt frustrated over the fact that she had devoted so many years of her life to raising her children who were now so distant from her. That deeply saddened her, but these feelings did not translate into outright anger until the night of a charity event which she attended about two weeks before her appointment with me.

There were a number of tables at this charity event. An old girlfriend, sitting at another table, suddenly stood up, practically ran over to her from where she was sitting, hugged Jayne tightly, and with tears in her eyes, sobbed, "Jaynie, Jaynie, I'm so happy to see that you're okay."

Jayne was very happy to see her friend, but was surprised at her tearful and emotional reaction. When she asked her friend why she was crying, her friend said "because you're alive! You're here! I can touch you!" This puzzled Jayne even more, until her friend's very next words, the words that had turned the hurt and the sadness that Jayne had been living with, into her fury. Her friend explained: "About ten days ago I saw your children in the shopping mall and asked about you. All they said to me was that you had died."

Needless to say, there are times when we find it understandable for a mother to cut her children out of her will. Sometimes, we might even want to say that the children cut themselves out of it long before the client reaches our office.

34. IMPORTANT BUSINESS

Graeme and Gillian came to my office in order to give me their will instructions. It took Gillian four months to get her husband, Graeme, to finally commit to an appointment date. Graeme was constantly dealing with his business affairs. Sometimes travelling, sometimes dealing with an emergency in the company, and other times tied up with some kind of business acquisition; he just could not give priority to making a will.

In our boardroom, Gillian was the first to speak. She hardly had time to talk about alternate executors when Graeme's cell phone started to buzz, vibrating the hard surface of the boardroom table. Graeme asked for a moment to answer his call, and I nodded in agreement. A moment turned into five minutes. Then our meeting began to progress some more, when Graeme's cell phone buzzed again. This time, Graeme was texting, even as Gillian was speaking to me.

From time to time, I could get Graeme's attention, but not all of it. Gillian, evidently a sensitive woman, whispered to me, "He's always like that. Sorry he's doing this to you, but he is busy with another acquisition. He loves making deals and making money. Don't ask me what it takes for me to get his attention!"

Our meeting dragged on, beset by multiple interruptions. More than once, Gillian would turn to her husband, "Got that? Got that?" Graeme would respond, nodding, "yeah, yeah, ok, ok."

I was comforted that this sophisticated businessman got the general drift of what we were doing, but it was very bothersome that his focus was just not where I needed it to be. Then a point came when I asked him something very specific as to what he wanted in his will. Still with his ear to the cell phone, Graeme waved his hand with a "go ahead" gesture, and said, "If I die, then Gillian will get it all, and the kids will take it all if she's not alive."

I looked at him. "Graeme, those are the wrong words." He looked at me, then looked at his cell phone as if it were a fourth person in the room. "Let me call you back," he spoke into his cell phone. Then his eyes swung back to me. Now his expression was challenging, as if his eyes were about to drill into me. "What do you mean, those are the wrong words?"

His cell phone calls had interrupted our meeting - a meeting that, in the long term, was probably more important than any other business call he could make. At that moment, it was my turn to interrupt him with a shot of reality. "Graeme, it's not IF you die. It's WHEN you die."

Immediately, upon hearing these words, Graeme's composure changed. The room turned silent as he just stared at me. His cell phone buzzed again on the table, but now, Graeme ignored it. He continued to stare at me in frozen silence.

I cannot recall how many seconds ticked by while Graeme continued to stare at me, but finally the silence was broken, when Graeme, still staring at me, slowly repeated the last words I had said to him: "WHEN...I...die..."

It took that kind of direct language from me for Graeme to grasp the fact that he was not going to live forever, making business deals, talking on his cell phone, and triumphing over his many business ventures. He may have thought that the amount of money to be made was endless, but with my continued dealings with people, I'm constantly presented with the fact that it's not the amount of money, but the amount of time that limits all of us - even the busiest, the most important, and the wealthiest.

35. WITH A COLD HAND

There are a number of ways that people receive inheritance money. Sometimes, as in Sonny's case, they have an appointment at the lawyer's office to sign some papers and to receive their money. What was so unusual about Sonny's situation was that he chose me as the person to whom he wanted to release some powerful emotions. This was Sonny's story.

Sonny was an only child who lost his father about ten years earlier and who now had lost his mother. He began by asking me what I thought of his smile. His attempt to smile revealed teeth which were very crooked, and in terrible shape. I couldn't understand why he was asking me to comment on his smile.

As he was signing legal documents, he looked at me and said, "My teeth are pretty bad, aren't they?" I didn't know what to say to him. I didn't want to hurt his feelings. Then he explained that what I was seeing across the boardroom table was pretty well the same as what the girls saw when he was a teenager. In those high school days, Sonny had begged his parents to take him for braces, but they refused. He knew that their clothing store was doing very well, and that they had the money to spend; but there was no way of persuading them to part with the cash to fix Sonny's teeth.

So, Sonny could not get a date for all of the years he was in high school. He was very used to holding his hand in front of his mouth, to cover his crooked teeth, whenever he happened to smile, or even when he was talking with friends. It became second nature to him. He was so ashamed of his appearance that he could not build up the courage to ask a girl out on a date. He was envious of his friends with straight teeth who had no trouble getting dates and going out and having a good time. There was one girl, Celeste, who so attracted him that he dreamed of asking her out. He pleaded with his parents to pay for the dental work that he so desperately needed. They still refused. It tore him apart to see Celeste in the halls walking with another boy. Sonny stayed at home the night of the school prom.

At least, Sonny was going to try to get a college education, and a good job, so he could find a way to pay for his dental work. But when it came to the money for college tuition, his parents refused, telling him that he would have to work it out himself. So Sonny decided to get a job driving a forklift in a factory for a year, to build up the money he needed for the college tuition.

The factory became his life. In the factory, no one cared about his teeth. His dream of going to college and becoming an architect began to fade. Also, he was getting promotions, and when he was made foreman who ran the whole factory floor, the idea of the college education, the profession, and his teeth were not as important to him as they had been.

After a few years, he met a woman who worked in the same factory. She seemed really nice, was friendly to him, and treated him with kindness. She was not attractive, but she was good company. They had enough in common to decide to marry. When it came to the wedding arrangements, he asked his parents to help

them out; but again, they refused. They would not spend a dime on the wedding.
They also told Sonny not to ask for help if he wanted to buy a house, because they
told him that the answer would be "no."

One year passed to the next, and during all of this time, Sonny never did get the
dental work done. His wife never pressed him on this, so he just let the entire
matter go.

Sonny went on to describe a very painful moment which occurred one evening
about four years ago. He was in a restaurant with his wife, when his eye caught a
couple coming in the front door. The woman happened to be Celeste, the same girl
who he had been crazy about in high school. For a brief second, their eyes met;
then Sonny dropped off her radar screen. She didn't give him a second look.
Suddenly, all of the old feelings came rushing back, along with the pain. Sonny
realized that somehow, life had passed him by, and that he didn't really love his
wife. He felt that he had married a woman who turned out to be his own
consolation prize. Right then and there Sonny realized that his life was going to
pass without the chance for real love and without any chance for him to realize
any of his dreams.

He then looked at the envelope which I had placed in front of him. "Is this what
my mother left for me?" Sonny asked. "It's $852,000 from your mother's estate,"
I said. He just looked at that envelope with as angry an expression as I had ever
seen. Such was his rage that his voice began to shake with his next words.

I held my silence, because Sonny's face had turned red. He looked up at the
ceiling, as if to address his mother. He thundered at her, "When I really needed
your money, it was never there for me! What the Hell do you want me to do with
this now? I'm seventy years old! You ruined every chance I had to get the girl
I really wanted! You wouldn't help me with college tuition! You said it was too
expensive, and that you couldn't afford it. Oh, yeah! Sure! You took away my
chance to get a profession or even get educated! I ended up spending the best
years of my life in a factory, just making a living! You chained me to a life where
not one of my dreams could ever come true. Now you decide it's time for me to
get the money? You can rot in Hell. Why didn't you just take your cold and dirty
money with you?"

Then, without another word, Sonny scooped up the envelope, shoved it in his pocket, and walked out the door, slamming it behind him.

36. WHAT SAM DIDN'T SEE

Sam had come out extremely well from his out-of-court settlement with his brother and sister, having taken the bulk of their late mother's estate. He felt that his siblings did not deserve the one-third share of the estate that they were claiming under their mother's will. He felt that he was a better child to his mother than either of them was. In fact, Sam felt justified in bringing up all the "dirty laundry" he could to present his case. After all, this was war. He had the money to pay his lawyers, and he knew that his siblings didn't. Both his brother and his sister caved in to his terms just outside the courtroom door, as he knew they would. Of course, this marked the end of any relationship with them. This didn't matter to Sam.

Sam's relationship with his wife, Tilley, also came to a bitter end, once Sam had finished with his brother and sister. Tilley was Sam's next victim. Tilley explained that her divorce settlement made only a dent in Sam's finances. Her comment about Sam was this: "Wolves aren't just satisfied with eating sheep for breakfast. They look for more sheep for lunch. I was one of those sheep. Sam was always good for preying on those who are weak."

She went on to explain that Sam's victory had alienated both her and their daughter. Neither of them would ever speak to Sam again.

All that having been said, about a year after the divorce was finalized, Tilley was surprised to receive a call from a hospital regarding Sam.

The hospital secretary told her that Sam had undergone major eye surgery and that the hospital policy prevented Sam from being released unless he was accompanied by another adult person. Tilley learned from the secretary that Sam had provided a list of names to the hospital, including his brother, sister, daughter, nieces, and nephews. The secretary said that she had called each and every one of them, and not one of them would come to get him. So, now she was asking Tilley. Tilley responded, "There is no way I, or anyone I know, would ever want to help that man. He made his bed. Let him lie in it."

Tilley wondered aloud to us how long Sam must have stayed in the recovery room, hoping he stayed for days waiting for anyone who would help him.

When we heard Tilley's story, we immediately recognized that Sam not only had physical eye problems, he had no ability whatsoever to "see" the negative effects his victorious battles for money would have on him in his future.

37. WE'LL TALK TOMORROW

Amalia came in to do her will in mid-December. With only a few business days left until the Christmas break, it seemed only natural for me to ask Amalia what her plans were for the holidays. To my astonishment, this innocent inquiry brought immediate tears to her eyes. "I have no plans. Christmas has become a very sad time of year for me," she said. I invited her to explain, if she wished to do so, and this is her story.

Amalia had worked as warehouse manager in Colin's wholesale car parts business. She described Colin as the perfect boss. She was part of Colin's team, and all of them took pride in the fact that they really knew what they were doing. The business had a good reputation and Colin's team was well-rewarded. Her pay was significantly above average. Colin never watched the clock, so if you came to work late, there was no problem. Of course, all of the members on Colin's team threw themselves into their jobs; and if they had to work overtime, they did it willingly for their charismatic boss.

Amalia said that, in a way, she even loved her boss. Aside from the generous salary she got, there were the gifts for her birthday, the bonus at Christmas, and also, the surprise little bonuses that were unexpected. The only strange thing about Colin was that, according to Amalia, he kept almost everything in his head. She described him as a very superstitious man. Colin had once confided to Amalia that secrecy about what he called "futures" had always worked for him. Only when a target had been hit, would Colin divulge details. Because of this aspect of Colin's personality, he was the only one who knew the inner details of the workings of the business.

Summer break was always a fully-paid two weeks. The Friday before summer break, Colin always threw a party for his team. And when it came to the Christmas break, that was also two weeks long; and the office Christmas party was even better than the summer break party.

Amalia then stopped telling me the details about all of the positive aspects of working as a part of Colin's team. She then turned her words to tell what happened one year ago.

Colin came to the Christmas party dressed as Santa Claus. He seemed so happy, and had something special to tell the team. As they settled into their meal, he said he had a special announcement. He had met a chemist who demonstrated a car polish the likes of which Colin had never seen in all of his years in the business. He went on to describe how the polish would take all of North America, and, maybe even the whole world by storm. Colin went on and on describing how it would bring the business to a higher level and how it would enhance the financial position of everyone on the team. However, all Amalia knew about this car polish was that it would be in their hands after Colin met with the chemist just after the Christmas holidays. Colin spoke of papers which would be signed early in the new year. So, everyone in the team was in high spirits. Amalia could not wait to hear the details of how they would get their hands on this car polish. She described her dialogue with Colin at the party:

"So? Tell me about this chemist. Where is he?" He reassuringly answered her with, "Tonight is party time. We'll talk about business tomorrow."

The day after the party was the last working day before the Christmas break. Colin had always arrived at the warehouse at eight in the morning. It was ten o'clock and no one saw Colin, nor had anyone heard from him. There was no word at lunchtime and no word at two in the afternoon. Amalia called his cell phone and his home phone and all she got was his voicemail. By three in the afternoon the team was altogether nervous about Colin. Then the call came from Colin's sister-in-law after four. Colin had suffered a fatal heart attack during the night.

As she related this part of the story, Amalia was sobbing. She loved her boss and knew that she would never again work for someone who was as dear to her. She continued with the sad ending. The young chemist that Colin had talked about was totally untraceable. Even after looking through all of Colin's records, there was no mention of names or contact numbers. She hoped that maybe the chemist might contact someone in the business, but no call ever came. The team very quickly realized that without their leader, there was no future for this business. Instead of the movement of the team to the higher levels that Colin had described, they had to find another option. It seemed at first that their best recourse was for Colin's executor to sell out to a competitor; then maybe Colin's estate might still have an interest in at least part of the business. The team reasoned that maybe this would still allow them to keep their jobs. Unfortunately, no competitor was interested in the business. The only other choice left to Colin's estate was to hold a liquidation sale for the inventory. What had seemed so valuable to Colin and the team so recently, now became bargain inventory to their competition.

Amalia described how shocking it was to behold that in less than a week, three forklift trucks could turn a warehouse into an empty shell. It did not stop there. It took only a day for the office furniture to go. It was especially sad for her when, for the last time, she looked at the carpet where Colin's desk had been. All that was left was the imprint on that carpet.

Amalia ended her story by saying, "It seemed as if life with Colin and the team would go on forever and not one of us realized how all of our careers depended on the life of the man we so loved and respected."

38. IN CASE

I arrived back at my office from lunch, to find a badly scuffed suitcase placed right in the middle of my desk. Attached to the handle of this frayed piece of luggage was a handwritten note which read: "Inside this bag you will find the two dead animals."

Immediately, feelings of dread arose from somewhere deep inside me. Who had I offended? What enemies had I made? I was shaken, and I sought the counsel of my secretary, whose common sense and practicality had backed me up so many times. "Call the cops right away!" she said. Her good counsel was to turn the matter over to the professionals who could best deal with threatening situations.

I was shaken to the point that I could not even make the call and I asked her to do it. Within thirty minutes or so, I found a uniformed officer in front of me with his notepad ready to take my statement. However, he wanted to commence his investigation by opening up that dreaded suitcase. I asked if it was absolutely necessary for me to be in the room. He suggested that, since it was my office, it was better that I remain. As he was unzipping the luggage, I was bracing myself for the odours and the horrible sights that had now gripped my imagination.

He laid the top of the suitcase open, and I am sure I must have turned beet red with embarrassment.

For a few moments I was entirely speechless. The contents of that old suitcase now jarred my memory of the purchase I had made a few weeks earlier from a friend of mine. He had been the executor of his aunt's estate. Since my wife was about the same size as his late aunt, I had bought two mink coats from him to give to her. My executor friend has this tendency to express himself as a comedian. It would be a serious understatement to say that I had fallen for his comical expression – once again.

39. THE CONFESSION

What does "winning" really feel like? My client, Russell, had a lot to say about how it really feels. In order to understand his story and his feelings, let us take a look at how he grew up with his brother, Wesley, and his sister, Vivian.

Russell and Wesley grew up as buddies. There was an element of competitiveness, but basically they got along. However, Russell had always adored his sister, and he would do anything for her. The feeling was mutual.

Their father passed away while the children were teenagers and still living at home. Mom had a large collection of crystal, silverware, figurines, and a few pieces of fairly valuable art. She had made a will leaving everything equally to the three children; but the will mentioned nothing about these particular items.

As the years passed, Russell, and then Wesley, married and moved out to start their own families. Vivian never married. She bought a condominium to live there on her own. Mom stayed on, living independently in the home where she had raised her three children. It came as a shock to Russell when Mom died.

As Vivian was arranging Mom's funeral, Russell was arranging for a truck to go to the house to take what he said Mom promised him. This may have been verbal, but Russell took her words as the authority to remove from Mom's home, all of the valuables that he felt belonged to him. He was encouraged even more, when Vivian told him she had no interest in taking any of the contents. Mom had given Vivian her wedding ring, and that was enough for Vivian. Russell was pleased to see that Vivian had it.

Wesley had been working out of town at the time, and had made arrangements to travel to the funeral. He had not been aware of Russell's visit to Mom's home until after the funeral. When he saw that the only remaining contents of the home consisted of furniture, carpet and minor ornamentation, he expressed his reaction through a letter from his lawyer. He demanded that the contents of the home be re-distributed so that he got his fair share under the will.

Russell responded to this through his own lawyer, refuting the claim advanced by Wesley. Russell relied on Mom's promise. His own lawyer told him that the case was a weak one, but Russell was adamant that Wesley would not put one finger on what Mom had promised him.

Legal arguments went back and forth, with a threat by Wesley that he would bring a lawsuit. Russell felt that Wesley was bluffing, and held his ground. After a year or so, Wesley backed down.

Meanwhile, all of those household items which he took from Mom's home were kept under the stairs leading down to the basement in Russell's home, packed in boxes. Victory felt as good to Russell as winning a fistfight had felt to him when he and Wesley had fought as boys.

None of the hostility between the boys had affected the close relationship between Russell and Vivian. She had always kept herself out of the actual fighting between the two of them. The fighting was stressful, and Vivian was always a source of strength and consolation to Russell. However, from time to time, she would remind Russell that they were all family, and it would be great if he could somehow get matters resolved with his brother.

With this background in mind, Russell described "winning" as the reward for determination…at first.

The rift between the boys was very deep, and neither of them had taken any steps to repair it. This state of affairs was fine with Russell, until one day, he got a call at work from his sister. Vivian asked if he could stop by her place on his way home. She had something to tell him.

She came to her front door when Russell rang the bell, looking pale and grave. Russell asked her if anything was wrong. She sat down on the living room couch and took off Mom's wedding ring from her finger. "This is for you," Vivian said. "I won't need it anymore." The news that settled first in Russell's head, then into Russell's heart, was that his sister was terminally ill, and at best, had only six or eight more weeks to live.

Vivian passed away. At her funeral, Russell was inconsolable. Wesley was also there to mourn her. He also loved Vivian. As both brothers were mourning the beloved sister they had lost, Russell realized that for the first time since he could remember, he had something to share with Wesley. At the gravesite, both brothers stood side-by-side. As Vivian's coffin was lowered to its final resting place, Russell turned to hug his brother. Wesley turned away from him.

Russell looked at Wesley, told him he was sorry, but Wesley's face was stone. After the service, Russell watched his brother walk away. Russell remained at Vivian's grave after the small crowd of mourners melted away. He stood there in the stillness. The only sounds which broke the silence were the two shovels of the cemetery workers who were now covering the coffin with earth. He must have stood there for half an hour, and then parted from his sister with, "I should have taken your advice." Russell didn't remember if he thought the words or spoke them out loud at her graveside.

"This," Russell told me, his voice heavy with sadness, "was when I learned about the sour side of winning."

After the funeral, Russell was determined to mend his relationship with Wesley, but to no avail. Russell looked at me and asked, "Has anyone ever told you that it was his or her fault? Has anyone ever told you that he or she had been the one to destroy the family?" I had to say to Russell that this was the first time anyone ever said anything like this to me. "I have to tell you that I thought I had all the answers, that I was always right, and that my brother didn't matter. Well, I was wrong. I caused this. Wesley did nothing wrong. I'm the one to blame."

"Mom's crystal? The pictures? The other stuff? They are in their boxes under the stairs in my house - just like they were left when I brought them to my house. I had to have all of this and the silverware. But we don't even use silverware in my house. All of this stuff is just sitting there in boxes. I had to have it at all costs, no matter what. Well, now I see the cost and I admit I was wrong. The stuff in those boxes destroyed my family, and I was wrong to do what I did." Russell decided that he was going to take a serious step toward fixing what he had broken.

Vivian's will divided her entire estate equally between her two brothers, and named Russell as her sole executor. Russell added his own instructions to us - giving their sister's entire estate - including his own half, to their brother, Wesley.

The gesture in and of itself was big. But the part that touched my heart was the note that Russell wrote by hand, to be delivered to Wesley when Vivian's estate was finalized. That note read: "Wesley, from the bottom of my heart, I am so, so sorry for what I did. Your loving brother, Russell."

We never heard how things turned out between those two brothers. What we do know, from our own experiences with family battles such as these, is that gestures like this do not always undo bad gestures from the past. Gaining possessions of coveted items like crystal, silver, and pictures can tear families apart. Sometimes, even if those items are eventually turned over to the losing party, families are not put back together, especially when so many years have passed between ownership.

40. THE TREASURE

I was in the process of buying a wedding gift in the fine china section of a department store, when suddenly I heard a crash behind me. Upon turning around, I saw a distraught woman bending over a broken cup and saucer that had accidentally fallen to the floor. I went over to help her, at the same time as a store salesperson. All three of us were bent over the several broken pieces as she said, "Don't sue me." I laughed and said that I would be more likely to defend her rather than sue her. She asked me if I was a lawyer; and when I told her I was a wills and estates lawyer, she introduced herself as Holly and asked if I wanted to hear a story about china treasures.

Holly spoke of her very long friendship with Willa. What Holly and Willa had in common was their love for figurines, fine china, crystal, and quality glassware. Holly had a few pieces, but did not have the budget to acquire very much of a collection. Willa, on the other hand, had inherited quite a few pieces; and then, over many years, had built up a substantial collection.

Holly spoke of how for years, every Saturday afternoon, she would be over at Willa's for tea. That was the time when Willa would tell the stories of how she built up her collection. She would pull out a piece, hand it over to Holly, and tell Holly everything about her life at the time the piece was acquired, as if it were a snapshot of that particular day, or that particular hour, or even a special moment in Willa's life. Holly never tired of these stories, even when they were sometimes repetitious. Holly knew that with every story, Willa would be admiring another piece, sometimes holding it up to the light. Holly described how she even enjoyed touching the smooth surface of each and every piece that Willa entrusted her to hold.

At this point in her story, Holly smiled and said, "No, I never once dropped anything. Nothing broke on my watch!" She then said that she had so much more to tell me. It was an estate story. She asked me if I would like to sit down for coffee, as there was a small cafeteria on the same floor as the china section. I was eager to hear more of what she had to say, so I agreed, provided that she would let me buy.

As we sat together, Holly's demeanour changed, as she described how tragedy came into Willa's life. Within a period of six months, Willa lost her husband and their only daughter. All the family Willa had left consisted of her two grandchildren, who were in college out of town.

Despite her tragic loss, Willa kept her spirits up; and, after a brief interruption, continued her Saturdays with Holly, almost as before. They still had tea together, and their attention was still focused on Willa's treasures. But as a widow, Willa now began to speak of the legacy she wanted to pass down to her two grandchildren who were now her only two surviving family members. She spoke of how she felt almost like a guardian rather than an owner of the treasures that were going to be given to her grandchildren after her death.

As time passed, Willa took advantage of occasions like Holly's birthday and Christmas to give several pieces to Holly; but it was clear in her mind that the treasures now had an appreciative home.

One day, Willa asked Holly if she would mind helping her wrap and mark the treasured pieces for the grandchildren. Holly knew that Willa had received some type of bad news after her last doctor's appointment. She also knew that Willa felt like time was of the essence now. At first, Willa and Holly would put away one saucer here, and one glass there, but it did not take long before the shine on Willa's shelves began to fade. Many of her pieces of crystal, glass, and bone china had found their way into Willa's drawers. Piece after piece was tightly wrapped in newspaper, carefully preserved for Willa's inheritors.

Willa had trusted Holly with her deepest secrets, and she even showed Holly her will. She was leaving a money gift to Holly, but the rest of her estate was to be divided equally between her two grandchildren. Also, the grandchildren were named as executors of her estate. The house was, of course, part of Willa's estate.

When Willa passed away, her two grandchildren came into town for her funeral, and this is when Holly first met them. They appeared to be in their late twenties. Holly had extended her condolences to them and offered them her help in any way they needed it. Although they thanked Holly, they kept their distance.

Shortly after the funeral, a "for sale" sign went up on the front lawn of Willa's home. All of this was happening just before Holly's vacation. She was going to the Caribbean for three weeks.

When Holly returned, she saw a huge refuse bin in Willa's driveway. She expected that it was there as part of the process of getting the house ready for sale, as now there was a "sold" label affixed atop the "for sale" sign. She also saw Willa's porch piled high with material of some sort, and she assumed that it was debris and garbage. Two men in overalls were working quickly. One of the men was pitching material from the porch into the bin, and the other man was moving material from the house onto the porch.

Holly went about her own housecleaning for an hour or two, and then went back out for some air. That is when she saw something that looked disturbing to her. The man on the porch was throwing some small items wrapped in newspaper into the bin. Immediately, she became concerned that the man was about to make a mistake. Holly knew what Willa had wrapped in newspaper and feared that somehow the man was getting into Willa's treasures. Holly ran into Willa's house. She wanted to stop the man inside from getting too close to the valuables.

She was too late. The drawers and shelves were empty. Holly asked the man in the house what happened to what was on the shelves and what happened to the items that were wrapped in newspaper. The man just shrugged. He just motioned to the man on the porch, who seemed to be the one in charge.

"Do you know what you are throwing out? Do you know how valuable these things are?" The man laughed. "Junk!" he replied. "What do you mean 'junk'?" she screamed. "I wrapped the valuables myself!"

Despite Holly's anger, the man continued to smile. "Look lady, if you want the stuff, I'll go to the top of the bin for you, and there may be something there for you; but the estate people went through all the drawers with me and told me to get rid of all of this. They said they had no use for any of it. They said it was all 'dust-collecting' junk."

"What estate people?" Holly asked. That was when the man on the porch described Willa's two grandchildren.

Holly's last hope was to salvage at least some memory of Willa from the bin. The man went down the stairs, placed a ladder next to the bin, and started to hand over some of the wrapped items to her. After shaking twenty smashed packages, and hearing the tinkle of the fragments they all contained, Holly finally was handed something that excited her. She shook a wrapped item and it sounded intact. Quickly, she unwrapped it and recognized the porcelain horse which had been one of Willa's favorites because she had bought it on her eighteenth birthday. Holly pulled apart the rest of the wrapping; and, sure enough, the horse was not smashed. But as soon as the last of the wrapping came off, so did the horse's tail. However, this would be the only piece of Willa's treasures that would serve as Holly's memory of her dearest friend.

Holly finished by telling me of her disgust with Willa's grandchildren. "Those grandchildren could not have cared less for what their grandmother worked so hard to leave them. Willa would be so hurt if she knew. Her heart would be broken just like her porcelain horse."

The saying goes: One man's trash is another man's treasure. Sometimes the opposite is true. In this case, one woman's treasures were her grandchildren's trash.

41. THE WISH

I happened to meet one of my clients, Armand, at the corner store where I was buying a newspaper. I asked him how it was going. He was just back from his trip to Florida, and he had a nice tan. He said that his cake shop was busy and doing very well. But Armand took me by surprise in telling me that he had received some very bad news from his doctor. Armand said that his prognosis was so bad that he wanted me to take a look at his will and his power of attorney, as soon as possible. He was diagnosed with a debilitating terminal illness that meant an irreversible decline in his health.

The words were hardly out of Armand's mouth when Bruce, one of Armand's cake shop customers, walked into this corner store to buy something. Armand introduced Bruce, who had a smile on his face. "Armand," he said, "You look great! Whatever you are eating or drinking, please tell me your secret. I hear you just got back from Florida."

As Armand nodded, Bruce continued, now looking at me. "You know," he said, "this guy's got a terrific business! He has the best cakes in town, and every time I go to his place, I always have to wait in a long line. Armand must be making a fortune!" Before either Armand or I could say a word, Bruce continued, "God, you look great, Armand; and you have the best business in town. I wish we could trade places. I wish I were you!" Bruce then paid for his newspaper and waved goodbye.

As soon as Bruce was gone, Armand, knowing how sick he was, and with no hope of improvement, looked at me and muttered, "He wishes he was me, but I wish I was him!"

42. A WILL AS A WEAPON

Henry described the fight he had with his sister, Miranda. Ten years ago, they did battle over their late father's estate. As hostile as this fight was, Henry had been pleased that the two of them were able to settle and avoid going to court. He was also very pleased with the terms of settlement with his sister.

In the years that passed, Henry was able to put all of the ill will and bitterness behind him. He invited Miranda to all of his family gatherings, and she had always accepted. Similarly, she always invited Henry and his family and they always attended. So, Henry felt that Miranda had forgiven him, in the same way that he had forgiven her.

Right up to the time of Miranda's death, he had felt that each of them had regained the love that they had for each other as kids.

However, nobody can really know the deep feelings which reside in another person. Often, such feelings are masked by social graces. This leads to the next part of Henry's discussion with me.

He handed me a copy of Miranda's one-page, handwritten will, which he had received from Miranda's executor. The will made provisions for various members of her family and a number of Henry's old friends who she had grown up with. She had dealt with all of the gifts in her will under two headings. The first heading read, "Gifts to those who I like." The second heading read, "Gifts to the ones who I hate." The provisions which were relevant to Henry and his family were under this second heading, and can be paraphrased as follows:

(a) To my bastard, evil, selfish, crooked, uncaring, piece of s**t brother, who lied and cheated his way through life, which included cheating me, I leave $1.52 to this thief because he doesn't need my money. He stole enough from me and from other people.
(b) To his witch of a wife, Gerda, who conspired with him to rip me off, and is as much as a fraud as her husband, and who dresses in fancy clothes which she bought with stolen money, I leave the cheap ring that turned my finger green.
(c) To the two offspring of these crooks, I leave one dollar each so they can buy a

coffee with the only honest money they will ever inherit because everything coming to them from their parents will be stolen money.

When Henry realized that everyone who was named in his sister's will would get a copy, he knew that they would all be reading Miranda's slanderous comments about him. He was angered and very concerned over the fact that his sister left very small sums of money to his friends, presumably to ensure that each and every one of them would be receiving a copy of his sister's will. He was in the financial services business, and comments like this could ruin him.

Considering that Henry thought he had made peace with Miranda, he was especially shocked by the depth of his sister's hatred, which she evidently had taken with her to her grave.

He wanted to know if he could sue his sister's estate for defaming his character. I had to refer him to a lawyer who practiced defamation law.

How does this story end? We still don't know. However, what we do know is that it would cost money, energy, and time to pursue a lawsuit of this kind. Maybe that's what Miranda wanted after all - for it to cost her brother - whether by using his money, energy, time, or defaming his character. I wish we could say that people don't use wills as weapons; but this is one instance where that's exactly what happened.

43. YOU CAN'T TELL A BOOK BY ITS COVER

Emma called in on a radio show to tell her story of sibling rivalry. She and her younger brother, Harvey, grew up together in a comfortable home. Their father had converted one of the rooms into a private library because he loved to collect hard-cover books. This library had shelves on all four walls; and over the years, those shelves were filled with these books.

As it turned out, the career paths and interests of sister and brother were very different. Emma devoted her time to the demands of her education, graduated medical school, became a doctor, and eventually, a specialist in her field. As for Harvey, he was a mediocre student, and never graduated from high school. Harvey bought a catering truck and sold sandwiches, soft drinks, and coffee to workers on construction sites.

Emma was very surprised to find out that several months after she bought an expensive new condominium with her husband, Harvey and his wife had, just like her, moved into the same building. From that point on, she felt that Harvey was competing with her. She and her husband each bought expensive cars, and before long, Harvey and his wife bought even more expensive vehicles. Emma was bothered by this and began to notice the watches her brother and sister-in-law were wearing, and the expensive leather jackets that Harvey and his wife seemed to be showing off. Where did he get the money to buy such expensive things? Surely it was not from the catering truck? Was Harvey's truck making him that kind of money?

After their father passed away, a copy of his will was given to both Emma and Harvey. Dad's will left his library collection equally to his two children. Emma had no feelings one way or another about this gift, but arranged a mover to pack one-half of the book collection in cardboard boxes. Harvey did the same. Emma had placed her share of the books in cardboard boxes in a storage locker in her condo.

One day, on a quiet afternoon, Emma decided to take a look at her half of this book collection, which she had ignored for pretty well all of her life. She pulled out several dozen books from their boxes, one-at-a-time, just looking for the names of the authors and publishers, dates of publication, and anything which might point to the possibility of value. In this process, she came upon something unusual. The spine of what appeared to be a book was entitled "Gulliver's Travels" but it was metal. She took "Gulliver's Travels" right out of the carton, and found it to be a locked metal box, formed in the shape of a hard-bound book, with a spine that looked like the spine of a book.

Her curiosity now aroused, Emma shook the metal box, but could not detect whether there was anything inside it. She saw a keyhole, but, of course, she had no key. At this point she was determined to find out what was in it. Her husband kept a number of tools, and she needed a hammer and a screw driver. Now, her only thoughts turned to the deep dark and potentially valuable secrets which the metal "Gulliver's Travels" contained.

She managed to secure the box so it wouldn't move, and, using a hammer, she smashed a screwdriver into the keyhole, and sure enough, the metal door of "Gulliver's Travels" swung open. A folded paper fell down onto the floor. There was nothing else in the box. She bent down to pick up the paper, opened it up, and read it.

It was a promissory note, showing Dad to be the lender. It was made out for half a million dollars, and all of the money had to be paid back to Dad. Her hand began to shake as she recognized the signature of the borrower.

She drew her mind back to the days when her brother, Harvey, had lived with Dad, and the way that Dad had supported him. That is the moment when she said to herself, "Aha! Now I've caught Harvey!"

It did not take Emma long to confront her brother about the debt that he owed Dad. She showed him the note that he signed, and the metal "Gulliver's Travels" that she had pried open. Harvey looked stunned. Then, Harvey swore that he paid Dad back. Emma didn't believe him. Half a million dollars from selling sandwiches off a catering truck?

"You see," she said, "I still talk to Harvey, but I don't trust him. There are no lawsuits, because I don't need his money. But I am getting sick and tired of Harvey trying to show me how rich he is. So next time he tries to show me an expensive gold watch or a new sports car, I have two words for Harvey, which should bring him down to earth, and make him realize that I know how he really got the money."

I had to ask her what those two powerful words were, as I was curious myself.

"Gulliver's Travels."

44. MOTHER AND CHILD

Mae was 97 years old when she came to our office to deal with an estate. She was a frail woman who walked with a cane. She appeared to be downcast, even heartbroken, as we began to discuss the business at hand, which was to deal with the administration of her daughter Violet's estate. Violet was her only child and had just passed away at the age of 79.

"I thought I knew what loneliness was, when I lost my husband, then my brothers and sisters, then, all of my friends. But Violet was always there to pick me up, and she was always there to look after me. She was my world. I didn't want to outlive her. It's not fair. But now that Violet's gone, my life is empty."

Mae's voice was shaking as she struggled with her composure. She continued. "You may see me as a sick old woman, but this isn't how I always was. I want you to see what I used to look like and how happy I used to be."

Before I could ask my questions, Mae said, "I carry my memories with me. I want you to see my darling Violet." With that, she took a picture out of her purse and put it on the boardroom table. It was a black-and-white photograph, which appeared to be very old. It depicted an attractive woman, with long curly hair flowing out of the cowboy hat she was wearing. She had a beautiful smile. She was standing beside a pony, holding its reins in one hand. With the other hand, she was holding the hand of a young girl who was also wearing a cowboy hat. The little girl was sitting on the pony.

She pointed to the beautiful woman. "That's me." She said. Then she pointed to the little girl. "And that's Violet when she was seven."

She put one more photograph on the table. This was a classroom picture. Mae had circled Violet's picture in pen. "This is Violet in the first grade."

It appeared for the moment that Mae had dealt with her pain, and I began my work by asking for her documents. The first one she put on the table was Violet's death certificate. But then she picked it up with her right hand, picked up Violet's class picture with her left hand, looked from the death certificate to the picture, and back again. Then she paused, looked at me with an incredulous, stunned expression, and said, "She was just about to turn eighty, and now she's gone. I can't believe I've lost my baby. What…am I…going to do…now?"

45. THE ITEMIZER

To best understand this story, a short family tree would be of assistance.

Cedric was 80 and widowed, and had two adult children. His daughter, Frederica was mother to three young girls. His son, Colby, was married and had no children. Cedric's existing will left everything equally to his two children, Frederica and Colby.

Cedric said that his family had always been close, and that he did his best to keep it this way. However, from what occurred a few weeks before our meeting, it became apparent to Cedric that his impression of familial peace was illusory.

What apparently triggered this problem was the free trip to Europe that Cedric offered to his children and grandchildren. His son, Colby, refused this offer. Frederica accepted the offer, and was thrilled to go with her family and Dad. This was not the first time Cedric had made this free trip offer to his two children. In fact for many years, Cedric had paid for family trips which Frederica had always accepted, and which Colby had always declined, because he disliked airplanes and travelling. As well, Colby's company gave him vacation times which did not line up with the annual summer trips which Cedric was in the habit of arranging.

It seemed that this time, Cedric's free trip generosity was the straw that broke the camel's back. It led to a very unwelcome reaction from Colby, which initially took the form of a list of expenditures that Colby had prepared and mailed to his father, Cedric. These expenditures dated back to the year 1982, and, according to Colby, everything on that list represented money which Cedric had spent on his daughter

Frederica or her children. These expenses were not confined to the annual trips, but also included Frederica's university education which had been fully paid by Cedric. Colby had chosen not to get a university education. There were many estimated restaurant expenses and birthday presents to Frederica's three daughters. There were expenses for the private schools which Frederica's three girls attended; these were also paid by Cedric. Frederica required a nanny to assist with raising the girls, and Cedric had paid for the nanny.

The expenditure list which Colby had prepared, continued with other miscellaneous expressions of Cedric's generosity to Frederica and her family, and even included trifling examples such as Cedric's payment for a clown at the birthday party of one of Frederica's daughters, and for tickets to a ballet recital for another of Frederica's daughters.

Needless to say, Cedric was stunned that Colby had kept a scorecard which itemized so many expressions of Cedric's generosity…a generosity which Colby clearly felt benefitted Frederica much more than him.

The itemized list, however, was not the end of the surprises which Colby had in store for his father. Colby called about a week after the list was mailed to Cedric, and asked if they could meet in a restaurant. "Father, you owe me at least one restaurant meal which Frederica doesn't share."

They met in the restaurant, and after dinner, Colby set out his demands to Cedric. The total of the gifts to Frederica and her family on Colby's list was over $100,000. "I think you have three choices, Dad, if you want peace in our family," said Colby. "Either change your will to leave me an extra gift of $100,000, or if you want a discount, give me $80,000 cash now." "What is my third choice?" asked Cedric. "Never see me again."

With that comment, Cedric left the restaurant, and left Colby alone to pay the bill. Cedric, in fact, decided that Colby's comment about changing his will was a good idea. However, this change would not take the form of adding an extra gift of $100,000 for Colby. Nor did it involve the discounted offer of $80,000.
The change would take the form of an entirely new will, one which completely cut Colby out of it.

46. I HEARD MY MOTHER'S WORDS

The call came to Fiona at ten o'clock in the evening. Mom was in the hospital! This did not make sense. Mom was a healthy 75-year-old, who lived independently in her own apartment. What was Mom doing in a hospital?

Fiona rushed down to the hospital. When she was led to Mom's room, what first met her eyes was an unconscious woman, lying on a bed, covered in a blanket, and hooked up to various tubes. This was Mom?

The attending doctor asked Fiona if they could go to a meeting room, as he had a number of issues to discuss. In their meeting, Fiona learned that Mom had been brought to the hospital by ambulance. She had fallen down the stairs leading from the street to the subway. Her injuries were severe. Several of her bones were splintered and she had already suffered a heart attack on the way to the hospital. The doctor went on to explain the serious domino effect which the accident had on his patient. Unfortunately, it all combined to result in the certainty of excruciating pain and an abrupt shortening of her life expectancy.

All of this was overwhelming for Fiona to hear. What made matters worse was the fact that her only sister, Alicia, was in South America and wasn't expected back for at least several weeks. She couldn't be reached by telephone or by email.

The doctor asked if Mom had any papers which might indicate what her wishes were in situations like this. Fiona didn't quite understand what the doctor meant. The doctor explained that a patient could sign a power of attorney directing the doctor what to do when situations as tragic as this one arose. He asked if Mom had ever signed one.

Fiona recalled having spoken about this to Mom in the past, but Fiona knew that Mom had never made a power of attorney document. She knew this because Mom would have not only told her, but would have given a copy of her power of attorney to her and to her sister, Alicia. As well, Alicia had never mentioned anything about one.

The doctor said that Mom's situation was very serious and that Fiona should leave her home phone number and her cell phone number with the nursing assistant.

He finished the meeting by telling Fiona that she should expect a call from him to update her.

Fiona went back to spend another few moments looking at Mom, then went to the nurses' station to leave her telephone contact numbers.

The next morning, the doctor called Fiona. He asked if Fiona could meet him again, that afternoon, at the hospital. There were no other details.

Fiona's instincts told her that the doctor had some very grave issues to discuss, and those instincts proved to be correct. The doctor explained in that meeting, that he was asking Fiona to make a life or death decision for her mother. Since there was no power of attorney which stated Mom's wishes, and since Alicia was not reachable, the guidance would have to come from Fiona.

Should she tell the doctor to extend Mom's life with medical equipment? According to Mom's doctor, that would mean prolonged unconsciousness; and if there were to be brief moments when she regained consciousness, those moments would be accompanied by excruciating pain and certain discomfort. On the other hand, should Mom be left in her natural state, without the input of the medical equipment? That would lead to a certain death within a very short time. But Mom's suffering would be minimal and brief.

Fiona was being asked to make a very hard decision. She loved Mom so much. A "yes" was bad, as was a "no." She had no legal papers from Mom to guide her, no one to lead her, not even her sister, Alicia. She found no comfort pacing the hospital floor, so she decided to take a walk outside, on the hospital grounds, to get some fresh air. Her walk generated memories. At first, the memories were scattered and random; Mom picking her up at school; Mom cutting her birthday cake; Mom taking care of her when she had a cold. Then she recalled the time when, as a little girl, she was in the kitchen with Mom and Alicia. Mom was washing dishes, Fiona was drying them. Alicia had opened the kitchen door for some fresh air. In an instant, Katy, their dog, leaped out that door, bolted out of a hole in the back fence, and before any of them could get to her, they heard the screech of car tires. All three looked at their beloved Katy, howling on the road. A car had hit Katy, and had completely run over her. The driver apologized profusely and drove them to the veterinarian. Katy was on Fiona's lap, whimpering. Fiona's jeans were soaked with Katy's blood, but all Fiona cared about was saving their beloved Katy.

The veterinarian's prognosis was very bleak, which brought forth even more tears from both Fiona and Alicia. Fiona looked at Mom. Mom always knew what to do.

"Mom, Alicia and I love Katy. We don't want to lose her. We've got to keep her alive as long as we can."

But Mom answered, "If you really love Katy, then you won't let her suffer." And with the recollection of Mom's words, Fiona now had the courage to take action on Mom's behalf. She now knew what Mom wanted, and what she had to tell the doctor to do about Mom's suffering.

47. THE COMPANY MAN

Alexander told us the following story about his father, Flynn. The moral of Alexander's story is that the footprint we think we are leaving in this world after we pass on is a lot shallower than we think it is. Alexander's story is recited in his own words.

"For over four decades, Dad worked for the auto parts plant, where he was the chief research and development engineer. I know that they had to have missed him when he died, because Dad always told me about the work that he loved so much. Even though he worked long hours and devoted most of his weekends to the needs of his plant, Dad always had time to answer my questions, and he always took time to explain his job to me.

At Dad's funeral, Mom and I stood beside Dad's friend, the manager of the plant. We all cried.

After the funeral, Dad's friend came over to our house to be with us. I'll never forget how he shook his head and told me that the only good news in his life, now that Dad was gone, was that he himself was headed for retirement within months. "Your father left a hole that will be hard to fill. But, I guess there will be new blood now," was his comment.

Dad's funeral was five years ago. Last week I decided to take my own son to visit the plant that his grandfather had devoted most of his life to building. Things had changed after Dad died.

The first change I encountered was the security desk. There never used to be one. I gave my name to the fellow behind the desk and he asked me to take a seat on one of the lobby chairs. Then, another man came out to the lobby. He asked me who I was and why I was there. I told him that I was Flynn's son. I told him that I wanted to show my son where his grandfather worked for over forty years. "Who?" he responded. "I'm talking about Flynn, your head of research and development who developed the products that you sell to pay your salary. I told him to ask for Rodriguez, for Walters, for anyone on the research and development team. The man looked at me like I had lost my mind. "You must have come to the wrong building, sir," he said. The names you describe don't work here. I asked him to call someone upstairs. Someone would remember Dad. The gentleman did as I had asked. While we were waiting for a response, I told him that Dad was one of the first employees of this company. Then the intercom buzzed and the man picked up. "No one here has ever heard of your father. I'm sorry for your loss and have a good day."

48. THE BEST MACHINE IN THE GYM

A client shared this joke involving a conversation between flabby, 70-year-old, Charlie, who was working out at the gym, with his trainer. Charlie was single, and had joined the gym in order to get into shape. Noticing a beautiful woman who was working out on a treadmill, Charlie asked his trainer if he knew her. "Oh, Yes!" said the trainer. "That's Susan. She's 45 and hot!" Charlie then asked his trainer for his opinion as to which machine in the gym would make him look good to her, and get her attention. "For you," said the trainer, "the best machine you can use to get Susan is the ATM machine near the front desk!"

49. THE BAGGAGE HANDLER

Marty came into the office in order to make a will. He wanted to leave his estate to the two daughters of his first marriage, whom he loved very much. He explained that he was now in a bad, ten-year second marriage and wished to cut his second wife out of his will. Marty then mentioned that he had never seen a lawyer to prepare a pre-nuptial agreement with her, or to get any other form of legal protection. I had to tell him that after he passed away, it would be very probable that his estate was going to be facing a battle with his second wife, for various reasons. This was not welcome news to Marty, who then wanted me to hear his story.

The path to his change of life started on a quiet Sunday afternoon. His life seemed boring, routine, and certainly was devoid of sexuality. He had been married for twenty years. Every day seemed to be like the day before. He ached for some of the excitement that he used to feel, earlier on in his marriage, and found it on a dating site on the Internet. Somehow, on-line, he "clicked" with another woman who seemed to have common interests, and wanted to have the same sort of fun and excitement that Marty did. One exchange led to another. At first, neither Marty nor the woman used their real names; but that changed one day when the woman asked Marty to call her. Her picture on the Internet was irresistible; her voice was sultry and soft. Her name was Belinda, and Marty was getting fired-up emotionally. He was ready to take a risk. They arranged a date in a downtown coffee house.

To say that Marty was overwhelmed would be an understatement. To him, Belinda was the ultimate woman that he had longed for, for many years. He immediately became infatuated with her. He wrote poetry for her. He sent her flowers and called her several times every day. But Belinda was an extremely attractive woman, and Marty was not her only male company. He confessed to pangs of jealousy whenever she told him that she was out on a date with another man. She was open with him because, after all, he was the one cheating on his wife, and she was a divorced woman.

As might be expected, all of this led to serious rifts in Marty's marriage. He had to make some decisions. He sat down with Belinda and she agreed that she would marry him once he divorced his wife. That is exactly what Marty wanted, but it came at a serious cost. He had to surrender the matrimonial home to his first wife, and to pay her substantial support. As costly as this was, there was yet another problem. In his rush to win Belinda's hand, he neglected to ask her to sign a pre-nuptial agreement. For this and the other reasons that Marty began to unfold, his comment to me was that his fantasy marriage to Belinda was the worst decision he ever made in his life.

According to Marty, one of the problems with marrying out of infatuation is that later on, you are going to discover many things about that person that you had previously overlooked. Belinda was a smoker. Not the casual smoker that he thought he had known, but a hard-core, two-pack-a-day smoker. She smoked inside their home, and even inside their bedroom. Marty called this "pollution" and they had fights about it. Belinda was a hard drinker, as well. Her attitude toward the house was disrespectful. Dirty, encrusted dishes were left on counter tops and on the kitchen table. The house was unclean. There was always a foul smell, either from the dirt, or the food, or the smoke.

Belinda had mentioned to Marty that she had a son in his twenties, who might visit them from time-to-time. However, prior to marrying Belinda, he had never met her son, and knew nothing about him. Within six months of the marriage, the son "came calling." He was a dysfunctional, unemployed drifter. He demanded money from Belinda the day he came to "couch surf," as he put it. After he spent the fifty dollars she gave him, he was back for more, with no indication that he was going to move on and leave her and Marty alone. She refused to give him the money and he flew into a rage. He smashed a glass table and pulled a light fixture out of the ceiling, leaving exposed wires overhanging the glass and littering the kitchen floor. He bent four kitchen cupboard doors backward and off their hinges.

She pushed him out of the house and he barged back in splintering the front door. Marty called the police; her son was arrested and charged.

Shortly after their marriage, Marty learned that Belinda was very poor at managing money. Before their marriage, she had run up a lot of credit card debt. When the bill collectors learned she was married to Marty, he began having to deal with them and organize a debt management program for her. Despite all the assistance Marty was giving her, Belinda continued to squander money. She had no problem running up new credit card debt for clothes and jewelry for herself. Her demands did not stop there. She wanted Marty to put the house and all of his investments in her name jointly with him, and also demanded that Marty give her two-thirds of everything else in his will.

Marty held his head in his hands and said, "Looking back, I never appreciated how good my old life was; and, now, I can never get that life back.

I really thought that marrying Belinda would bring back my youth. After the first three months with Belinda, there was no excitement or fun. There was yelling, screaming, and slamming down phones. The stress of this miserable marriage has turned me into a sick old man. I was caught by surprise by all the baggage Belinda was carrying with her.

I can't afford another divorce. All that's left ahead of me now is to be an old baggage handler. And, boy, did Belinda come to me with lots of baggage. What would I give to go back to what I had with my first family?"

50. THE COUSINS

Eighteen months had passed since Grandma had recovered from the heartbreak she suffered when each of her two children tragically perished while they were on vacation. Her son and his wife, together with her daughter and her husband, had left for a skiing trip, during which all four of them suddenly lost their lives.

Each of the couples had left one child. Ethan was her daughter's son, and Chelsea was her son's daughter. The two young cousins were staying with Grandma while their parents were to be away for ten days. Now ten days had become forever, and Grandma was in our office to change her will so that she could appoint a guardian to raise young Ethan and Chelsea, who were currently in her custody.

Grandma's feelings about what now remained of her little family led her to make one comment that will stay with me for a very long time: "I'm going to leave a note to the guardian that I have raised my grandchildren, Ethan and Chelsea, not as the cousins that they are, but as a brother and a sister. I want to make sure that my guardian does the same, when I'm no longer around."

51. THE HOSPITAL VISIT

At a financial planning seminar, the topic was about baby boomers suffocating in debt. That led to informal discussion among the attendees; and from that discussion, we heard the following joke.

It was Levi's 57th birthday, and he was not having a good day. He had just received some heavy credit card statements in the mail. However, as bad as Levi's day was, his father was having an even worse one. He was sick, and in the hospital.

Levi's problems were financial. He was living the "good life" but his income came nowhere close to supporting his lifestyle. He stuffed his credit card bills into his briefcase as he drove to visit his ailing father in the hospital.
Unlike Levi, his father had no financial problems. A wealthy widower, he would never be able to spend even the interest on his investments. But Levi's father's problems were medical. He had severe asthma, compounded by a lung complication. When Lance arrived, Dad was in bed, under the covers, and a breathing mask covered the lower half of his face.

Levi stood back from the bedside and thought, "I'm his only child and he's hanging onto all that money." But to Dad, Levi exclaimed, "Dad, I hate to see you like this! I love you so much…Watching you like this is tearing my heart out…You mean so much to me…What can I do to help you? I'll do anything to make your life easier."

Dad turned his face on the pillow to get a better look at Levi standing there. Slowly, Dad pulled his arm from under the bed sheets, and with trembling hands, he pulled at the mask that was covering his mouth, at the same time as he motioned Levi to come nearer to him. As Levi came close to Dad's face, he exclaimed, "Dad what is it? I'll do anything for you. Please tell me how I can help you!" Dad finally managed to pull the mask off of his face for a second, and said, "Get your damned foot off my oxygen tube!"

52. THE CASH COWS

Nelson and Clara, an elderly married couple, both using walkers, had come in for their will appointment. They said that they were very upset with their only child, Lance, and they wanted to cut him out of their wills.

They told me that they had just come back from an exhausting trip. They had travelled a very long distance by train to visit Lance, who was in his late forties, and lived in a small, mining town. This was the first trip they had taken in many years, and they were exhausted. The only method of travel to the mining district was by train, unless you had a private plane.

I was imagining how difficult that trip must have been for them. What crossed my mind at that point was the image of Nelson and Clara getting by with their walkers in a rugged environment. However, I am getting ahead of myself. This was their story.

Their son, Lance, was very obese. He had been a loner, and had no friends.
With the financial help and guidance of Nelson and Clara, Lance graduated from college with a degree in geology, but he could not get a job.

For many years, unemployed Lance lived at home, and was supported by Nelson and Clara. Tension grew between parents and child to the point where, in an effort to defuse this tension, Lance said he was going to leave and live on his own. It was to the small town in the mining region, that Lance had made his move. It made sense to Nelson and Clara that Lance would move there, because he would have a better chance of employment as a geologist in a mining region. But once Lance had settled into his new living arrangements, it did not take long before the telephone calls they began to get from their son expressed his feelings of depression. They would hear statements from their son along these lines: "I'll never get a job in my profession. People here are so prejudiced. Fat people can't get a job up here."

For a number of years, Nelson and Clara continued to support their son financially. In their telephone conversations, which were frequent, Lance would describe how difficult his life had become. Among his many complaints, Lance made it clear that his obesity was impairing his health and well-being to the point that he required expensive medications.

Eventually, Lance told them about his only friend, a woman who herself was burdened with disabilities. Lance described how much the two of them had in common, most of which turned on the desperate living situation which the two of them shared. Lance also told his parents that he was marrying this woman, but that the ceremony was going to be private, before a justice of the peace. Lance did not want his parents to have to travel a long distance on the train for this. Despite their protests, Nelson and Clara yielded to their son's wishes, and they did not go north to see their son get married.

Just before Nelson retired, he had arranged for a very large line of credit on the home he owned with Clara. They felt that whatever Lance and his wife might need, they would provide. They were concerned because Lance and his wife both had medical problems, and would probably need a lot of help. If their pension money was not enough to cover Lance's needs, then the line of credit would provide borrowed money to fill the gap. And, as events turned out, the gap had become a very large one.

Nelson and Clara missed their son, and wanted him and his new wife to visit; but Lance kept putting them off for one reason or another. Usually, it was either a bout of ill health or lack of money. In these conversations, Lance was always sure to mention that a job seemed to be just out of his reach.

Lance eventually announced that he and his wife had a baby boy. Before long, what Nelson and Clara heard was that their young grandson was a child with special needs. Accordingly, in every conversation that followed between parents and son, the subject of money came up, first and foremost.

Nelson and Clara routinely sent Lance the money they were borrowing on the equity of their home; and all the while, they continued to miss their son. They wanted to see their grandson. They wanted to meet Lance's wife. Finally, they came to a decision. If Lance was too sick, too poor, and too overwhelmed to come to see them, then Nelson and Clara would pay a surprise visit to him, no matter how difficult the trip up north might be.

As they had expected, their trip was not easy, but the trials and inconveniences of travel paled to what Nelson and Clara found when they got to the little mining town.

They had checked into their motel and decided that they would surprise their son. Next, they took a taxi to Lance's apartment. When they arrived at the apartment building, they were pleased to see that it was better than what they had imagined. They pressed the buzzer for Lance's apartment and were allowed in. They were also pleased that the apartment was on the first floor, as their arthritis and their need for walkers would have made it impossible to go upstairs. When they knocked on the door of Lance's apartment, a woman opened it, asking who they were. Nelson and Clara identified who they were and then asked if the woman was their daughter-in-law. "Not at all," she laughed. "I'm the nanny your daughter-in-law hired." She then went on to explain that Lance and his wife had just left for Puerto Rico to take a ten-day cruise. They had just left the day before, and the nanny told them how bad she felt that Nelson and Clara had missed their son and his family only by a day. However, she showed them around the apartment. It was lavish, and very well-furnished.

Nelson was narrating this to me, and, at this point his face had turned very red; he was shaking, and visibly angry. "Here I was, for years, supporting what I believed was a sick family with my borrowed money. We mortgaged our home for them. Meanwhile, the nanny was telling us that the two of them were working in the district office of one of the large mining firms. He was the head geologist of the company. She was the company's chief accountant. They each drove nice cars. Neither of them had any health problems, and Lance had lost almost all of his excess weight. Our grandson was in no way a special needs child, like Lance had told us. I saw a picture of the three of them near the dining room table. We've been fooled by our own son. He must think we are stupid!"

Clara added that she and her husband had worked so long and so hard to make money and to save it. What they saw in Lance's home was the squandering of what they had worked for all of their lives. She seemed to be as angry as Nelson was. "We mortgaged our lives for our ungrateful son. We were heading for the poorhouse. He obviously couldn't wait for us to die. He wanted his inheritance now, and lied to us to get it. Well, all he is going to get is a letter from us telling him that he milked us enough. He won't get a nickel from our wills!"

53. HAVE YOU TOLD YOUR CHILDREN?

On a radio show, our host put out the following question to his audience, wanting their comments: "If you have cut a child out of your will, or have left him or her less than the others, have you told that child?" We heard some intriguing reactions, which we will now share with you. We will paraphrase the comments of the callers:

1. If I tell my son now that he isn't getting as much as his sisters are getting, he won't be shocked later. His sisters will need the money much more than he will. He married well.

2. What I'm doing in my will is not any of my daughter's business. I earned this money. She didn't. Where did her sense of entitlement come from? Do I have to tell her how much I spent at the grocery store, or how much I gave her brother for his birthday gift? Should I reward her for rarely visiting me?

3. I lost my son because I was open with him and told him that I'm leaving more to his disabled sister. He's a successful professional and she can't get a job. He yelled at me, cursed me, threatened me, and ran out of my house slamming the door behind him. But, so be it, I've got to protect my daughter who needs my help.

4. Forget about cutting out one kid. After my divorce, I cut all of my kids out of my will. I left everything to my new wife, who is good to me. She was there for me day and night when I had open-heart surgery. They never came to see me or even called. They didn't care if I lived or died.

5. I have to admit that maybe I went too far, but I told my son that he will only get an inheritance from me if he divorces his wife. She brought poison into our lives and destroyed our family.

6. My son has been terrible to me. He refuses to let me see his children. He hasn't spoken to me in ten years. My friends tell me that he talks badly about me behind my back. If he'd answer my calls, I'd be thrilled to tell him that he is cut out of my will. He has caused me such anguish and heartache that I mailed a copy of my will to his house. Assuming that he read it, he would have seen that his sister would get my whole estate, and he could read the reasons why, which I spelled out clearly in the will.

7. We had a family meeting. My five kids all told me to cut them all out of my will, and that I should leave everything to their children, to give them a head start in life. I have to tell you that not one of my kids' husbands or wives were invited to our family meeting, because we all know that they would never have agreed to our estate plan.

8. This is what I told my kids: You all came out of my womb and each of you will be getting an equal share of the money. But, you should know that your eldest

sister is the only one who I trust to be an executor to look after my estate when I'm gone, and that is how it's going to be. Too bad if you don't like it.

9. Imagine, I have four children who don't seem to give a damn about their sick mother. I have Parkinson's and heart problems. My eyes are bad and it's hard for me to get around. You'd think that one of my children might come around to visit me but they're all too busy with their own lives. They don't deserve to inherit from me. The one who's really looking after me is the care-giver I hired. She looks after me the way I should be looked after, so now I'm looking after her. I may be sick, but I am rich; and she's getting it all when I pass on. I know that all four of my kids are thinking "Windfall!!" when I die. But they are in for a shock. You know what? I want to surprise them!

10. I would love to sit down with my kids and tell them what I have in my will, but I'm afraid of a volcano erupting. So, I decided not to tell them anything, and to let the volcano erupt after I die.

11. Of course, I had to tell my daughter that my son is getting the business. He is the one who worked there most of his life. My daughter never stepped foot in there. My daughter thanked me for telling her. She said she never expected any part of it, and she is not at all upset. I know that telling my daughter what she's not getting will make it easier on my son after I die.

12. I really should leave my son less money. I told him, more than once, that he would get less than his sister from my will. I know that if I leave an equal part to him, he's going to blow it. But he is a sixty-eight-year-old, doesn't have much to his name, and I can't bear the thought of hurting him. I have to leave him an equal part. I won't try to control him from my grave. Life is too short.

13. I felt a sense of relief after I met with my kids to sort out what they would get from my late wife's jewelry and my own valuable collections. I made the final decisions on this, and not all of them were pleased. But my only comment to them was that if they love me, it must be for who I am, not for what they are going to get.

14. I will tell you what is not automatic. Just because something belongs to Mommy or Daddy doesn't mean that Junior is going to get it. My parents left all they had to charity, not to me, and I'm going to do exactly the same thing.

15. When Mom was close to the end of her life, she told me that my stepdad was a good man, and that she was going to leave everything she owned to him when she dies. She assured me that he would look after me when he died. He assured me this, as well. But, I knew I'd never get a red cent from that man. Sure enough, he died last month and left everything to his own kids, including everything my Mom left him. He cut me out, just like I knew he would. That's okay. I'm a proud person and can make it on my own. But Mom shouldn't have trusted that man the way she did.

54. FOUND MONEY

We are used to hearing stories about sibling warfare in our wills and estates seminars. Greed, aggressiveness, insensitivity, and various other negatives form a common thread in the narratives that we hear. Against this background, what made Evan's story so surprising and so memorable was his relationship with his sister, Leona. She was with Evan when they both came to meet us at the end of the seminar. This is a paraphrase of what they had to say, in the presence of each other:

Evan: "I've heard a lot about the bitterness between brothers and sisters tonight, but I have to tell you that I can't relate to these people. I love my sister and I know how much she loves me. She is a saint. Do you really want to know the kind of person who is standing beside me here? When she found that bag of hundred dollar bills in the air duct when she was cleaning Dad's home after he died, she could have kept the money. But, instead, she brought the bag to me so we could share everything in it, and there was a lot of money in that bag."

Leona seemed embarrassed with this comment. Evan continued, turning to his sister, "How many people here tonight would do what you did, Leona?"

Leona: "I'm not a saint. A lot of people I know think I'm a fool. I've actually been told that I could have and should have taken the money and not tell Evan about it. How could I? That would be stealing from my brother. What those people told me is disgusting to me. If something belonged to Dad, then it belongs to Evan and me together. Believe it or not, I have to say that sharing the money with Evan gave me more pleasure than I would have had if I had kept it from him."

55. CAN I HAVE YOUR PHONE NUMBER?

Trevor walked into a bar, looked across the room, and saw a gorgeous woman. Trevor went over to her and asked if she was alone. She was. He introduced himself and just felt compelled to impress her.

What began to catch her attention was when he said that he was an only child, and, therefore, heir to a massive fortune.

He told her about his father's great wealth, his mansion, his ownership of so many companies, and the two yachts in Bermuda that his father owned. He said, "My dad is 89, a widower, and when he dies, it will all be mine!"

Now having captured the attention of this gorgeous woman, Trevor asked her if he could have her phone number.

"No," she replied, "but can I have your father's number?"

56. HIS LAST WISH

This is the joke we heard at another seminar.

Harry's days were numbered. Sophie, his wife, had been spending every day in his hospital room for weeks; but now the doctor had told her that Harry could pass away at almost any time. So today, Sophie knew that this might be her last chance to tell her husband what was in her heart.

"Harry, we've been married for 60 years. I know that I have nagged you, caused you a lot of grief, bothered you too much, but I love you. I blame myself for causing your first heart attack, with all the stress I caused you. I know that I almost pestered you to death. Even though I threatened to leave you so many times, I want you to know that I have always loved you. The doctor just told me you don't have much time, so I am asking you if you have any last wish. I want to do whatever it takes to give you a little happiness."

Harry looked at her with a smile, and said, "Sophie, just promise me that right after I die, you will start a relationship with my ex-boss, Norman. I want you to date him a few times and then marry him as soon as possible. I know that when I was working for him, he told me how much he liked you, and I think he still has feelings for you."

"But Harry," replied Sophie, "I thought you always hated Norman so much that you quit working for him."

And Harry said, "Yes, Sophie, I still hate him!"

57. AFTER THE FIGHT (ONE): GOOD-BYE!

Jerry walked up to his brother, Lawrence, in the courthouse parking lot. After six years of heavy litigation which Jerry initiated against younger brother Lawrence, a failed attempt to mediate, and six gruelling days in court, the judge ruled that Lawrence won. It took all of this to show Jerry that he never had a case against Lawrence.

Jerry to Lawrence: "I know we went through a lot, but as far as I'm concerned, I want to put this all behind us. I should never have started any of this. Mommy wanted us to be close, and we were always close when she was alive. Starting a lawsuit against you was really a big mistake on my part. Between my money problems and my bad marriage, I had too much stress on me and you were just an easy target.

You were right all the time but I just had to hear a judge say it to me. I lost the case and I accept it. You won and I also accept that. I am so sorry that I brought you into this legal mess. We have many years left to be good friends again, so let's let bygones be bygones, and look forward, not backwards."

And with that Jerry put out his hand. Lawrence nodded his agreement and the two brothers shook hands.

Lawrence to Jerry: "I understand everything. Yes, you made a mistake. You had your day in court, and we'll pretend this never happened. We'll be in touch."

That conversation took place many years ago. It was the last time Lawrence ever spoke to or saw his brother.

58. AFTER THE FIGHT (TWO): THE PAYBACK

At the conclusion of the first day of a two-day workshop on wills and estates, Marcus said that he had a story about what he had experienced many years ago, as a result of a court victory over his siblings, regarding his father's estate. He wished to share his story with us. He said he wanted to show us some unusual family correspondence in his possession. When he came to the office the next day, he brought the correspondence with him. He wanted us to see an example of what can happen to a family that was once close, and how family secrets can come back one day to haunt and even betray a person. As you will see, he had his reasons for feeling as he did. For the subsequent events he described to us, Marcus never retained a lawyer, and the matter never went to court; but the situation bothered him for many years. The following is a narrative which approximates Marcus's story.

Fighting off six siblings who took him to court over Dad's will almost drained Marcus's resources, but his court victory over all of them made Marcus feel euphoric. This court victory gave Dad's valuable farm to Marcus, free of any claims from any of his siblings.

If ever there is a good day of the week to win a serious court case, Marcus would tell you it's a Friday. For an entire weekend after his victory, he was on cloud nine.

His joy, however, was short-lived. By the following Thursday, he found that someone was defaming him. His boss called Marcus into his office and closed the door. He pulled out a letter and gave a copy to Marcus. The letter read, in substance, as follows:

To the Boss of my Brother, Marcus,

1. So, you think Marcus is a university graduate? Think again. If he showed you a degree; it is a fake. He never wrote his second-year exams. He quit the university because of his drug addiction. The only exams he ever wrote were first-year exams.

2. He knows how to pull off a swindle and hide it. You better check your bank books because a lot of your money is in his bank account. How do you think he paid for the swimming pool in his back yard?

3. When you visit his house, look for a supply of pens, sticky notes, binders, and photocopy paper - reams of it. It all belongs to your company.

Sincerely,
Marcus's sibling

Because of that letter, his boss put him on probation for three months until it turned out that the allegations in the letter had no substance. Marcus was then hired back fulltime, but lost three months of sleep, and had to see a doctor to prescribe him anxiety medication.

During the time that he was on probation from these work problems, Marcus was watering the grass at his house, when his closest friend, from across the street, came over with an angry expression on his face. He slapped a letter into Marcus's hand. Without a word, he turned away and headed back across the street.

The letter read, in substance, as follows:

To Marcus's friend across the street,

If your wife is named Marilyn, ask her why, when you were away on your last business trip, Marilyn went to expensive out-of-town restaurants with my brother. And, ask her how she likes the watch he bought her and how she likes her blue dress, which came from my brother, also. You should also ask her why she gave my brother a personal tour of your bedroom.

Marcus gave you a couple of compliments...He liked your bedroom linen, your expensive cognac, and the big walk-in closet in your bedroom. But, he felt the shower stall in your master bedroom was a bit too small for his taste. I'll leave the rest of what happened to your imagination.

He also said that as much as he liked Marilyn, he didn't like you. You were always in the way and he wished you would go for another long, long trip.

Sincerely,
Marcus's sibling

A few days after the interaction with his friend from across the street, he got an angry call from his fiancé. Her voice was like ice. She wanted Marcus to explain a letter she had just received.

Marcus raced over to her house. She showed him the letter (which Marcus kept). It read, in substance, as follows:

To my future sister-in-law,

You ought to know that you are engaged to a lying, cheating, sick, uneducated crook. He is about to lose his job. He is about to lose his closest friend.

When you are planning a wedding, you should invite Marilyn, his best friend's wife.
I hear you are rich. Marcus always said he only wanted you for your money.
He has other women, including Marilyn, to go to for his other needs. Hope you get a pre-nuptial agreement.

Sincerely,
My Brother's Keeper

Marcus said that he was at a loss as to whether these letters came from one sibling, or from two of them, or from all of them. He had trusted his brothers and his sisters with a lot of his personal information when they had been close; but his court victory over his siblings made Marcus realize what a serious mistake he had made by confiding in them.

When it comes to dealing with your siblings, his message is to hold your tongue, because you never know if what you tell them will be broadcast to the whole world, in an attempt to hurt you. Marcus could live with the lies which were told about him. But he was destroyed by his family's abuse of his trust. Marcus's bottom line was that he kept his job, but lost his best friend from across the street, lost the girl he wanted to marry, and from all the heartache caused by his bitter siblings, probably lost a few of the best years of his life.

59. AFTER THE FIGHT (THREE): THE TIGER

Cyril's opening comment to his story: "Have I been blind all these years?"
He then spoke of his brother, Mason. Even though Mason had been the school
bully, Cyril always looked to him for protection.

From childhood on, Mason seemed to get what he wanted by making threats.
At first it was to classmates, then to teachers, then later in life by starting lawsuit
after lawsuit. If he didn't like a product, he sued the manufacturer. When he was
an employee, he ended up suing his boss. His motto was: "I have my rights."
Mason even bullied their father to let him into the business. Cyril followed Mason
into the business, although Mason's share was larger than Cyril's.

Until now, Cyril always looked up to Mason. He even sided with Mason when
their father passed away and Mason successfully went to court to keep their three
sisters out of the business. Cyril faithfully contributed to the legal fees. Cyril felt
that he was on his way to a lucrative partnership with his brother. But Mason's
next move was to force Cyril out of the business with a buy-sell procedure.

Cyril's comment after being forced out of the business by Mason was: "I fell into
Mason's trap, didn't see this coming, but should have. My brother is an animal
who devoured everyone who came near him. Now he ran out of people to devour,
so he decided it was time to eat his former best friend and ally…me!"

60. ON A SAD NOTE

Ricardo was a background singer on the stage, playing to the evening audience
of the theatre production on our cruise. The day after we heard him sing, we
happened to meet him on the deck, and we introduced ourselves. When he heard
that we dealt with wills and estates, he became very talkative, as if he knew that
he had found willing ears to hear his life story. He started by saying that he had
recently made a will, but added that he had very little to leave, and very few

people to benefit from him leaving it. Just before starting his story, Ricardo said, "If I could turn back the clock, and change just a few minutes of my life, I know that I would be a rich man today!" After that exclamation, Ricardo told us his story, paraphrased as follows:

"My band was formed in 1967 and we were on the right track from day one. We would be famous now if I had done it right. But I didn't. I wrote the lyrics, played the guitar, and sang background vocals. At the high school and college dances, they couldn't get enough of us, especially the girls."

Pictures show a lot, and Ricardo took out a handful of pictures, which he had kept in his wallet. Some of the photos showed a young Ricardo with his band, and, others had him posing with over a dozen men and women who had become very famous in the music industry.

But of all the pictures he showed us, the most striking was Ricardo with a young woman with long blonde hair, tied with a tie-die bandana. In a word, she was beautiful. He could see our reaction, and his mood turned melancholy. He continued:

"That's Hannalea in 1968, after one of our outdoor concerts," he said. "She was my lover, my muse, my everything."

He went on to describe how she was, at first a groupie, turning up every time the band played anywhere. Then she became a friend of the band. All five band members agreed that their music and their careers would be paramount, and no women or love affair would throw them off the track.

Through 1968, the band made a lot of progress, and played as a warm-up band at many concerts for very famous groups. They caught the attention of the record industry, and, by the time 1969 came around, they were one of the groups to be invited to a major pop festival. "The highs and lows of my life occurred in 1969," said Ricardo. "The highs were that my band was on its way to stardom, and that I was the man who wrote all the words of all of the songs. As well, I fell in love with Hannalea, although this broke the band's most important rule. But, I was convinced that the band needed me more than I needed them, and I wanted her.

Just look at her. Hannalea inspired me. I always wrote with her in my heart. But now that she was mine, I wrote a whole piece just for her. I was flying."

But, the four other band members didn't like all of the words in that song. They felt it was too personal and just didn't like it. "They said, if I wouldn't change it, they wouldn't play it. Some of the lines were inspired by Hannalea, and I promised her I would use them. They said they hated the lines, and if I didn't change the words, they would can that song.

But I was Ricardo, and there was only one of me. I said I wouldn't change one line of that song. They said that if that were the case, they would never sing it. So, I said, 'I you don't sing it, then I quit!' But the one thing I never expected was when they responded with, 'See ya!' So, I split with them. But I still had Hannalea. Or, so I thought. After being out of work for four months, I saw her personality change, and before long, she was with the lead singer of a successful band from England. So, I lost her, too.

A couple of years later, I ended up getting back with the boys, and we re-formed the band. But now our gigs were few and far between. The music world had changed, and no one cared any more about our band or our music. We knew we were washed up, so we split.

So, to make a living after the band broke up, for a while I sang background on commercials, sang at some malls, played background guitar here and there, and wrote lyrics for some children's records.

Now here I am at 67 years old, with arthritis that won't let me play the guitar, and I am singing background vocals in a cruise ship show.

I'm happy to have the work, don't get me wrong, but no one is screaming "Ritchie! Ritchie! Ritchie! Like they did when I was hot; and no one is waiting for my autograph when the show is over. I guess I can thank my ego for this."

61. MOM'S GRAND-STRANGERS

I was working out at the gym beside Ronen. He told me that he had seen me on television a number of times, and he knew that I was a wills lawyer. We then took a break from our workouts so that he could tell me his story.

In order to understand Ronen's story, a brief family background will be of assistance. Ronen was unmarried, and had been living with his widowed mother for many years. Ronen was companion, care-giver, and best friend to Mom.

His only sibling, Jay, passed away years ago from a heart ailment. Jay was survived by his wife Marcia, and two very young children, Abigail and Spencer.

At the time of Jay's funeral, and for a short period after that, relations between Mom and her daughter-in-law, Marcia, were cordial. The two grandchildren, Abigail and Spencer, were very young.

As Abigail and Spencer were Mom's only two grandchildren, she loved them very much. According to Ronen, Mom never quite got over the loss of her son; and she often told Ronen, "Jay's kids are all I have left of him." But Mom's feelings were not mirrored by her daughter-in-law, Marcia. Mom's requests to visit with her grandchildren, Abigail and Spencer, were often met with excuses. The time gaps between Mom's visits to Marcia's home grew longer and longer. But this was not due to Mom's lack of effort. Mom constantly sent gifts for birthdays and other occasions, but rarely got thanked. All of the telephone contact took place because it was Mom calling Marcia's home; but Marcia never initiated any calls to Mom.

None of this dampened Mom's feelings for Abigail and Spencer. She loved them, and Ronen spoke of her constant hope and expectation that when they got a little older, they would love her, and they would be a family with her. But from Marcia's point of view, Mom's calls became intrusive and unwelcome, even to the point that Marcia said to Mom, "Can you stop harassing us? These are my children, not yours, and you will see them when it's convenient for me, not when it's best for you."

Ronen said that it did not take Marcia very long after Jay's death, to form a new relationship with another man, and then marry him. Mom was not invited to the wedding. Marcia, the kids, and her new husband moved to his hometown which was thousands of miles away.

All Mom ever got was a note formally telling her of their new address. The note also warned Mom that surprise visits were not welcomed, and that she should not visit at all unless she was invited by Marcia. But no invitation to visit was ever sent to Mom.

After all of this, it did not affect Mom's feelings about Abigail and Spencer. Ronen loved his mother, but when more than a dozen years had passed with no meaningful contact with either Abigail or Spencer, he felt that their ongoing silence should have told Mom that the relationship that she longed for with her grandchildren would not occur.

However, this was Ronen's thinking, not Mom's. She was unfailingly convinced that her own warmth and generosity to Abigail and Spencer, even at a very long distance, would one day be rewarded. For this reason, she had done her will and had told Ronen that because they were her son's children, she was leaving "something" to Abigail and to Spencer, so that the efforts she was making during her lifetime would not be foreclosed by her death. Ronen was respectful of Mom's wishes, but felt that she was deceiving herself.

It was not until Mom passed away, about six months before I met Ronen, that he learned of the "something" that Mom had left her two grandchildren.

The way the "something" came out was at Ronen's meeting with Mom's lawyer. There was no formal "reading of the will" like you see on TV. The meeting consisted of the lawyer showing the will to Ronen. The lawyer explained that Ronen was named as executor. He had to look after paying the bills, the taxes, and then the rest of the estate was divided. Abigail would get twenty percent of the estate; Spencer would also get twenty percent; and the rest would go to Ronen.

At the lawyer's office, Ronen took this in stride. The "something" did not seem to be particularly threatening; and perhaps, at this point, he thought that these gifts to Abigail and to Spencer might be the very step that needed to be taken in order to bring them back to the family, although with Mom gone, Ronen became the last of what Mom used to call "family."

Aside from his meeting with the lawyer, Ronen's first step was to make contact with Abigail and Spencer. His wish was to give them the news of their inheritance with as much warmth as possible. However, with the passage of so many years since his last contact with Marcia and the kids, he felt that the best way to let them know about their inheritance was to send them a letter in care of Marcia. He had posted a letter to them a few weeks before Mom had passed away, telling them, at the time, that Mom was very ill and that she would love to at least have a phone call, a few words, from her grandchildren. She didn't impose a request to actually visit her, just wanted to hear their voices. But all Ronen received from the letter was silence. At least the letter did not come back "return to sender," so he knew he had the right address.

Ronen put a fair amount of thought into the way he would set up his "about your inheritance" letter. He felt that once Marcia saw where the letter was coming from, she might just toss it out without even opening it.

Since this was Ronen's one and only opportunity to extend a welcoming hand to his niece and nephew, and since the warmest words he was capable of writing would only be read if the envelope was opened, he took the precaution of writing on the back of the envelope, in large black script "INHERITANCE." He also made sure that he inserted his telephone number so that they could contact him.

This worked. Ronen succeeded in getting the attention of his niece and nephew, who said they would book a flight right away and come to see about the inheritance. Ronen suggested that they wait about a month so that he could organize Mom's estate and be able to let them know approximately what they would get.

The phone call was cordial, and when a month later Ronen answered the doorbell as Abigail and Spencer arrived for their visit, the first thing Ronen told his niece and nephew, was how much of their late father he saw in them. They thanked him, and over coffee, they told their uncle about university life. Ronen told them how much he loved their father, and expressed over and over his hope that they could be a family again.

The visit was still cordial, until Ronen started to tell Abigail and Spencer how much their grandmother had loved them. He pulled out a photo album and wanted them to see pictures of their late grandmother, and perhaps they might want to keep a couple of them. But Spencer retorted, "No way! My mother always told us what a rotten bitch she was, and how she constantly pestered her! Forget it!" Abigail added, "Yeah, I heard what a nasty one she was!"

As distressed as he was to hear such words about his mother, Ronen kept at the front of his mind that the point here was to re-connect with the closest thing to a family that he knew. Still, Ronen had to defend Mom's reputation. He began by telling Spencer and Abigail how their grandmother was a gentle, caring woman who devoted her whole life to her two sons; however, he saw his words were not having the effect they were supposed to have. Ronen could tell from their body language, the looks the two of them exchanged, and the shaking of their heads that they just didn't care.

Ronen went on to say that he had devoted his life to looking after their grandmother; that no one knew Mom better than he did; and that he was her care-giver, friend, and companion for many years. He told them how much their grandmother loved them, and how many nights she stayed up worrying about them. That is why she gave so generously to them in her will, even though she had not seen them since they were little kids.

That led to the following exchange:
Spencer: "What did she leave us?"
Ronen: "Well, she had some investments that your grandfather left her, and two bank accounts, a few government bonds, and some gold jewelry, which we will split up among us."
Abigail: "OK, but what does that mean in money?"
Ronen: "I would estimate that each of you will get about $50,000 each."
Spencer: "That's it? That's all we get?"

Any remaining cordiality between the three of them was now dissipating by the minute. Both Spencer and Abigail were intent on sweeping everything in sight into their grandmother's estate. They were firing their challenges at their uncle almost as fast as their eyes could take in the furniture, the sterling silver in the cabinet, and even the pictures on the wall. Ronen would hardly be able to answer one of them, before the other put forward his or her next pointed question. Ronen bought this or that piece with his own money and it didn't belong to Mom. "Prove it!" Ronen described the gold jewelry. "How do we know that you didn't take the good stuff already? What are you hiding from us? The large screen TV?" Ronen told them that Mom bought it for him for his fiftieth birthday. "Yeah, sure! We want proof!" said Spencer.

Anger was now building on both sides, but it came to a head when Abigail quipped, "And what about the house? Didn't your mother own it? We own almost half of that from her will! And we want you to sell it! We came for our money!"

With that, Ronen finally lost his patience, saw that there was no way to establish any kind of a relationship with these two, and now it was his turn to retort, "So you come here after all this time to put me on the street? You can go to Hell. Get out of here!"

The two of them left, convinced that they had found treasure. Ronen never gave his answer to the two of them, until he received their lawyer's letter demanding that the house be accounted for in the estate. That is when Ronen went to his own lawyer to give his answer.

Mom may have been generous to her grandchildren, but as much as she loved them, she loved Ronen more, and many years before, Mom had protected him completely by putting the house in Ronen's name. So when she died, the house already belonged to Ronen.

Ronen was now coming to the end of his story. He made this final point. Mom went to extraordinary lengths to show her love to her two grandchildren who she had lost sleep over, and all she got in return was their silence. "My mother worried for so many years of her life over these two greedy devils? They couldn't have cared less about her, and she's lucky she never lived to see what they turned out to be. She would have been so ashamed of them!"

62. CRUEL SISTER

Amy tirelessly did her best to look after Mom.

Months turned into years, as Mom gradually declined into an almost helpless state. The physical and emotional drain, after so many years, began to take a toll on Amy, to the point where her doctor insisted that she take a vacation from her care-giving duties so that she could recharge before her own health started to deteriorate.

It was the doctor's advice that led to Amy's call to her sister, who lived out of town. The distance had so far cushioned Amy's sister from all of what Amy had to live through.

It was Amy's call to her sister that brought out the difference between Mom's two daughters. Amy was a loving, caring daughter. But her sister was not.

Amy: "Can you come to Mom's for two weeks? Mom's not well and right now I'm so drained that the doctor told me I have to get away. I want to book a cruise with my husband as soon as I can. I need to get some sun. I need to unwind."

Sister: "Don't you understand? Why are you killing yourself for her? She's 92. What do you expect? She won't live forever. I have my own life, my appointments, my business functions; I'm on the board of a charity. I have my personal trainer, my show tickets. I can't just drop everything and cancel all this. I have my own life to live. Why don't you just hire somebody to look after her? And, if it is money you're calling for, then I'll give you what you need. Just say how much! And, if you're really calling for me to pay for your trip, I'll do that, too!"

Upon hearing this response from her sister, out of pure disgust, Amy threw the phone down on the floor so hard that it broke into pieces. She never spoke to her sister again.

63. A SELFISH COMMENT

"After Dad died suddenly, I took a few weeks off work to recover from the shock. I was deeply depressed over his loss. We were so close to one another. When I came back to work, I told a co-worker that my heart was broken because I never had a chance to say good-bye to my father. But instead of consoling me, this person's shocking response to my loss was, 'You're so lucky! You didn't have to look after your father like I have to do. His heart keeps ticking like a clock, and meanwhile, I have no life of my own. Who knows how long it's going to go on for me! It could be years!'"

64. THE CARE-GIVING CONTRACT

The radio call-in show topic dealt with aging parents and care-giving children. From the various calls that came in, we selected the following memorable exchange:

Caller to radio host: "I'm going to tell all elderly parents out there how to get your kids to look after you when you need their help. In my case, I'm cooking, cleaning, and shopping for my mother. I take her to the doctor, the dentist, and the chiropractor. I told her I wanted to get a weekly salary for helping her this way. So, I made my mother sign a contract to pay me for doing these jobs."

Radio host to caller: "Are you kidding me?"
Caller to radio host: "Why should I do this for free? I'm not her slave!"
Radio host to caller: "Maybe your mother should have charged you for looking after you when you were a kid! I think you owe her a lot more than she owes you."

65. THE PLANNER'S NUGGETS

A financial planner shared with us some of the stranger experiences that had come from his practice.

For a 95-year-old, optimistic client, the planner arranged for a ten-year treasury bill because this client insisted on investing for the long-term.

Another client refused to be named as beneficiary on his wife's insurance policy. When pressed for a reason, the client told the planner, "Because if she dies before me, I don't want to be accused of killing her!"

The planner could not resist adding one more interesting client comment. When setting up an investment file, he asked his client how old he was. The client's response: "In my head, I'm 18. In the mirror, I'm 81!"

66. THE TURN-OF-THE-CENTURY WILL

Gary told the following story to us during a call-in show. His father, Percy, made his will at the height of the dot-com stock market surge. Percy's stock portfolio was worth over five million dollars in the late nineties. He wanted to divide his growing estate among his many friends, his relatives, and his two children, of whom Gary was one, and Denise was the other.

It was important for Percy's children to have the lion's share of the estate, because they were his only children, and, particularly because Denise was ill with multiple sclerosis.

Just before making his will, Percy consulted with Gary and Denise, explaining that after he passed away, because of the value of his stock portfolio, they would each be so wealthy that they would never have money problems. But there were numerous others who really needed financial help, so that his will would contain many smaller gifts of money to those others.

Gary, out of serious concerns about the medical and therapeutic needs that would arise over the lifetime of his sister, Denise, asked Percy what he meant by "numerous others." Percy explained that counting all of his friends and cousins, there were twenty people, and each one would get $10,000. A total of $200,000 didn't seem like a lot of money out of a total stock portfolio worth five million plus at the time, so Percy had the blessing of Gary and Denise, and the will was finalized along these lines.

By the time Percy passed away, Gary learned three hard lessons. First, he learned that five million dollars' worth of Internet stocks did not translate to five million dollars of currency after a stock market bubble bursts.

Second, Gary learned about which gifts in a will get paid out first, and which gifts are only paid if there is money left over after the priority gifts are paid. The sad part of this lesson was that Percy's friends and relatives got their money gifts first, leaving Denise and himself to split whatever was left after those money gifts were paid out. This followed the wording in Percy's will, which provided that Gary and Denise would split what was left over in Percy's estate, after the money gifts were paid out to his friends and relatives.

Third, Gary learned how thankless people can be when he realized that Percy's net worth after debts and taxes was only $230,000. This meant that after the two hundred thousand dollars were paid out to Percy's friends and relatives, Gary and Denise were left with $30,000 to split between them. What was the thankless part? Gary talked himself hoarse, begging Percy's relatives and friends to give up their gifts so that the money could help Denise deal with her illness. He made a point of telling each of them that Percy would never have left his sick daughter in such a vulnerable position. Percy wanted to protect her. But not a single one of Percy's friends or relatives agreed to consider Denise's needs. Not one of them would give up their $10,000 gift from Percy's will.

Gary's said that he and Denise were raised as givers, not takers. Gary gave all of his $15,000 inheritance from Percy's estate to Denise, and more beyond that out of his own money. And what he had to give to the radio audience was one piece of advice to anyone making a will. Just because you're rich today doesn't mean you'll always be rich.

67. OUR LITTLE SECRET

We were hosting a radio talk show about caring for elderly parents. Estelle was too nervous to make a call to tell her story over the air; but the situation she had lived through was something she had to get off her conscience. After the show had concluded, Estelle called the producer and asked to speak to us "off the air." This is what Estelle had to say.

She had twin daughters that she referred to as, "Desiree the evil one," and "Kim, the good one." Estelle said that her daughter, Desiree, implemented a cruel and devious plan to get Estelle to make a will so that Desiree would inherit Estelle's home when Estelle died.

Estelle described how Desiree had lost her job, and with time on her hands, would visit with Estelle almost every day. On all of these visits, without exception, Desiree would engage in a constant sequence of antics to convince Estelle that she was losing her mind. For example, "Mom, you left the fridge door open all night;" or, "You left the stove element on all day and it's a good thing I was there to shut it off;" or, "Thank goodness I was there to close the tap on the bathtub, Mom; you left the water running and it almost overflowed;" or, "Mom you keep calling me Kim, but I'm Desiree, remember?"

Estelle, recalling that her own mother had Alzheimer's, and constantly hearing Desiree emphasizing to her, how dangerous it was for Estelle to live on her own, eventually started to believe that she was in the early stages of that disease. It was at this point that Desiree made her sinister arrangement. Desiree told Estelle that if she would make a will leaving the house to her, Desiree would keep the Alzheimer's a secret from everyone. Furthermore, she would move in with Estelle and look after Estelle for the rest of her life. But Estelle would have to make her will quickly, before her disease worsened. Finally, there was the pact between mother and daughter. Neither of them would speak to anyone of Estelle's secret disease, or about Estelle's new will.

At this point in time, Estelle was very vulnerable. So, when Desiree brought a will form home to Estelle, Estelle felt she had no choice but to sign it. She did sign it in front of two of Desiree's friends who Desiree brought with her to be the witnesses to Estelle's will. Desiree's plan worked. At least, it worked up to that point.

The next Thanksgiving, Estelle's other daughter, Kim, the good twin, came to visit from out of town. It did not take long for Kim to suspect that her mother was holding something back from her. Between mother and daughter, it did not take long for Estelle to break down and let the secret out. "I think I have Alzheimer's" Estelle confessed to Kim. Kim had her doubts, and started to ask Mom questions to test her capacity. She asked Estelle questions such as, "What's my husband's name? What are the names of my kids? What is your phone number? What is my phone number? Where do you do your banking? Who is your doctor?" When Estelle answered all of these questions quickly and perfectly, Kim went on with more questions, which now addressed the distant past. Who were Kim's homeroom teachers in grades nine and ten? Estelle knew their names. She also knew who taught both girls biology, chemistry, and the grades they both received in those courses.

At this point, Kim made arrangements to stay in town to get to the bottom of this so-called Alzheimer's problem. She got Mom to a capacity assessor who found that Estelle had one hundred percent capacity. After that appointment, Kim asked Estelle why she felt she had Alzheimer's in the first place. It was right at that point, that Desiree's plot became clear to Estelle. As she turned her mind to the various incidents and events of the last several months, she could hardly believe that Desiree, her own daughter, her own flesh and blood, would mislead her by turning on taps and stove elements, mumble incomprehensible sentences, and prey on her deepest fears, all to make Estelle think that she was losing her mind. It became crystal clear to Estelle that she could not possibly have been the confused, aging mother with signs of dementia that Desiree suggested she was.

The next event to unfold was when Estelle went to a lawyer who prepared a proper will, revoking the one that she was pressured to sign, leaving Desiree her home. Her final comment to us: "I think you can figure out which twin is getting my entire estate, and which twin was thrown out of my house!"

68. LOOSE LIPS

We had given an estate planning seminar, and, during a question-and-answer session about locating the assets of a person who passed away, several people offered opinions, which went all over the map. One person found it useful to look at old tax returns to see if there had been any dividends paid throughout the years. Another person suggested looking for important papers in the freezer, because that is what he had done in his situation. Another person said that it was almost impossible to know where the deceased person did his or her banking, unless there were clues; and these clues were in the strangest of places. This person found these clues inside shoes and shoe boxes, gym bags, jacket and pants pockets, kitchen drawers, and vases. Another person was frustrated because he had no password to his cousin's computer, which contained the entire portrait of his estate.

That comment seemed to pale in comparison to the next one, where a woman complained that after her brother passed away, she used her brother's key to get into his home. The burglar alarm immediately went off, and she didn't have the pass code or the security password, and the police were summoned, leaving her to do a lot of explaining.

Gerard provided the most surprising story about how he discovered one of the assets of his deceased father, Harry, by simply being a good listener. The following is his story.

Gerard, his sister, and their families came to Harry's funeral in a limousine that had to be parked at the side of the cemetery roadway. After the burial service was concluded, they were the first mourners to get back to their parked limousine. The weather was very warm, so one of them had opened one of the heavily-tinted windows about three-quarters' of an inch. Due to these tinted windows, nobody walking by this limousine could see inside it; and since its engine had not yet been started, it appeared to look as if no one was inside it. Of course, from inside the limousine, Gerard, his sister, and their families could see everything and hear everyone who walked past it.

Aside from Gerard, his sister, and their families who were in the limousine, everyone else had to walk past the limousine in order to get back to their cars, which were parked in another area of the cemetery. Among the remaining mourners returning to their vehicles, were Gerard's cousin and his wife, who were slowly walking past the slightly-open window of the limousine. What Gerard overheard his cousin say to his wife, led to the comment about being a good listener:

"It's a good thing that Uncle Harry died so fast, because we can now breathe easy about the eighty grand we borrowed from him! No one will ever know about this. It's all ours now, and we'll never have to repay it!"

Gerard concluded his comments to me by saying that until he heard these words from his cousin's mouth, he had no idea about the loan that his father, Harry had made to his nephew. As a result, Gerard sent his greedy cousin a thank-you card for attending the funeral and for making his father's estate $80,000 richer. Gerard was Harry's executor and was now determined to collect the eighty thousand from his cousin who had the loose lips.

69. THE MOST BEAUTIFUL WOMAN

When Ivan made a call to our radio show, the discussion had turned to people dealing with personal possessions in estates. Many callers spoke of fights over various items such as cherished family heirlooms. Others spoke of compromises they had made. But, Ivan had a very different and touching story to tell all of us on that radio show.

He said that he was a graduate student in an art college. At a gallery showing that was conducted at the college, he met a doctor who was interested in certain portraits which were being displayed; and, the two of them began to talk. They quickly discovered that they shared a love of artwork; and, the following week, they met for coffee. From these two early encounters, they developed a friendship; and one day, the doctor invited Ivan to visit him after hours at his office, as he had something important that he wanted Ivan to see.

When Ivan arrived at the doctor's office, the doctor was still attending to his last patient; but the doctor's assistant showed Ivan to a small room where he saw the backside of a painting. It was not hanging on a wall. In fact, it was on the floor, leaning at a propped-up angle against the wall.

The doctor's assistant then said, "The doctor wants you to look at this painting," and, then she left him alone in that room. When Ivan turned the painting around, it portrayed an indescribably beautiful woman. Ivan was deeply moved by this work of art. It was love at first sight; and, Ivan said that he had rarely experienced such emotion in looking at a portrait. The woman in the painting was leaning against a bridge, a strong breeze playing with the strands of her flowing hair. Hoop earrings captured the sunlight. Ivan was overwhelmed by her image.

After about ten minutes, the doctor entered the room. Ivan began by telling the doctor that he felt totally captivated by this work of art. Ivan asked the doctor if this was what the doctor wanted to show him. Ivan also had to know if the doctor had any idea of the woman's identity in the painting. It was then that the doctor held up his hand to stop him from any further inquires.

At this point in my conversation with him, Ivan began to describe the exchange between himself and the doctor, more or less along the following lines.

The doctor: "The woman in the painting looks so very much like my late wife. It was on our honeymoon when I bought that painting from an art gallery in Paris. I had to buy it because it was the image of the woman I have never stopped loving. Ever since I lost her, I have not been able to look at the painting because it breaks my heart. I needed to take it out of our home; so, I took it to my office until I could find it a new home, where her image could bring some joy to the right person. We never had any children and I have no family. I could never take any money for it. That is why I thought of you. I know that you will find a special home for her."

It was then that Ivan realized that the doctor, who now had tears in his eyes, was about to give him this incredible painting.

Ivan's story stands out in my mind against a background of people squabbling over possessions left in estates. In this doctor's case, he had exchanged a cherished possession for a chance to have peace. This was the doctor's way of finding closure.

70. THE BALLET DANCER

Jessie's story is about someone I have never met; however, this is a person who certainly touched my heart.

It was during our first meeting that I had asked Jessie, a new wills client, what she did for a living. She said that she was a registered nurse who worked in a nursing home. She told me that while she is working there, she sees a side of life which is very different from the "work-hard, play-hard" life that so many others may be used to living. To the residents at this nursing home, the hands of the clock mean very little.

Over a span of twenty years, she had seen so much tragedy, so much sadness, that the faces, the stories, the personalities all seemed to blend into a world drained of color. One person would pass away, to be replaced by another, and then another, year after year. The satisfaction she was able to gather from her circumstances were from trying to help these people cope with and deal with what slivers of life were left to them. I began to sympathize with her, when she added that there are times when some of the people she looks after do have a significant impact on her.

As she told this, she became animated and said that the faces of these people, and their stories that they had, would stay with her for as long as she lived. She went deeper into her life descriptions as she began to tell about Chantal, a former ballet dancer who lived in the nursing home, and who had become very close to Jessie's heart.

Chantal was a paraplegic in her sixties. She was an only child, who never married, and had no children. She had lost both of her parents some years before. Her legs had been impacted in a tragic accident, and Chantal would live the rest of her life using a wheelchair. When Jessie first met Chantal, what Jessie saw was a pleasant, attractive, but rather depressed woman, who appeared to have no interests in anything in particular.

One day, a woman came to visit Chantal, carrying some packages, and asked for help because she wanted to hang various items on the wall of Chantal's room. Jessie agreed to assist this woman, but first wanted to know what it was that the woman wished to hang on Chantal's wall.

The woman explained that she used to be in the same ballet company as Chantal, and, that they had performed and danced together for years. She said that Chantal was extremely talented, and one of the items she had brought was a framed award that Chantal had been given after a standing ovation at a performance recital.

The friend also brought with her a ticket stub from that performance and a picture of Chantal and this woman taken in their ballet outfits. Finally, there was a much thicker frame inside of which the woman had placed Chantal's worn ballet shoes. All of these were beautifully framed behind glass.

The friend strongly felt that hanging these items on Chantal's wall would have an uplifting effect on her. So, Jessie got the permission from the nursing home and helped the friend hang all of these items on Chantal's wall.

What was the effect on Chantal? At first, she seemed to be captivated by the framed items, and, for the next few days, Jessie noticed a smiling face that she had never before seen on Chantal. However, when Chantal began to talk to Jessie about "those good-ole days," the smiles soon disappeared. After that, whenever Jessie went into Chantal's room, she would find Chantal sitting intently next to the window. Chantal would eat some of her meals looking out of that window, and would stare out of it, as if her eyes could absorb the entirety of the outside world.

One day, when Jesse was with Chantal, they were both looking out of her window. Suddenly, a squirrel jumped from a tree onto Chantal's window ledge. Then the squirrel jumped from the ledge and onto the branch of a nearby tree.

Chantal turned to Jessie, and said, "I wish I was that squirrel. It is so free and can do whatever it pleases." Then, Chantal's right arm rose to the window in a movement so graceful that Jesse knew that Chantal was reliving a magical, ballet moment. Chantal's long fingers traced an arc against the window. She slowly turned to Jessie and said, "I want to dance again, but I know I never will. She then turned to what her friend had framed on the wall and said, "I am like my old ballet shoes. We are both trapped forever behind glass."

In the span of those brief moments, Jessie saw her life from a different perspective. I was so touched that I knew it would affect my perspective on my own life, as well. To Jessie, it was important to dictate her will for the "ballet shoes" and other treasures in her own life. However, Jessie's real lesson was learned from her daily visits with Chantal in the nursing home. She learned that the real treasures in life are sometimes the things that we did in those "ballet shoes," and not the ballet shoes themselves.

71. INHERITANCE GUILT

Josef and his brother, Peter, were signing papers in order to administer the estate that was left to them by their widowed father, Klaus, who had recently passed away. Josef and Peter were Klaus's only children. Josef was fifty-five, and his brother, Peter, was fifty-eight. Klaus's will named both of them as executors, and he divided the estate equally between them.

As related to me by Peter, he and his brother were very close to each other and to their father. They were very saddened by his passing. In fact, if Josef had appeared to be depressed by this loss, Peter was absolutely heartbroken. This is what Peter had to say.

Klaus was a butcher by trade; and he ran a very successful butcher shop. Peter and Josef spent the first years of their working lives in that shop, working part-time while they were still in high school. Subsequently, each of them went on to college. Then, Peter went into the insurance business while Josef became a salesman. Each of the brothers decided not to take a part in their father's butcher shop business because it required a gruelling devotion neither felt they had for it. However, those early years were deeply etched in Peter's memory. He described what life was like in that store.

If a good butcher starts his day the way Klaus did, the working day started at five-thirty in the morning. Business actually started well before the first customer of the day walked in the door. The meat had to be purchased from the wholesaler. When the cows, the pigs, and the lambs came out of the refrigerated delivery truck, the entire portions of the animals could be seen hanging on large, steel hooks. There were rails on the ceiling of the truck which matched the rails in Klaus's store. The steel hooks slid along those rails, from the truck, right onto Klaus's rails, which led to the meat cooler. The cooler was kept at a regulated temperature, and it was lit by ultraviolet and fluorescent lights.

Then came the real work. Klaus would hack the meat into ribs, shoulders, steaks, his butcher knife cleaving into the animals as if he were a precise diamond-cutter. Blood and parts of entrails stained his apron, his shirt cuffs, his hands, and his fingernails. Klaus would wash all of this away several times a day, to ward off infection and contamination of the precious meat. His hands were often cut, and he had lost a finger in that very meat cooler several years ago.

Then there were the customers, of course. There were also the chickens, which were another story altogether. Klaus was at the store for six-and-a-half days a week. Many years ago, his wife passed away, and then the six-and-a-half days turned into seven.

Right up to the year before his death when he sold the business, life for Klaus consisted only of that store. Peter knew that his loving father sold his life's work in order to spare his boys the task of winding up the business. Josef added that his father knew no pleasures throughout his life. There were no trips, no nights dining out at restaurants, and no going to see movies. There were no family cars. The only vehicle in the family was Klaus's truck.

Josef went on to describe his father's life in four words: a life of sacrifice.

It was, therefore, no surprise to the boys that the estate was worth well over two million dollars. Included in the estate was the family home which had been mortgage-free for a very long time. There were also the many investments and the various bank accounts.

Peter appeared to have unburdened himself after having shared his views of Klaus's working life. The business of administering the estate proceeded without incident from that point onward. In the end, Peter had an inheritance which exceeded $750,000.00, as did his brother, Josef. For most brothers, this would have been the point of the story where the file would have been closed.

However, the emotional and personal aspects of this story begin about nine months later. Josef called to make an appointment with me, and showed up for our appointment with his brother, Peter. Josef's appearance had changed over the passage of those months. His face had aged and he was now balding.

Josef's voice had become hoarse. It was evident that he needed this meeting. He needed to put a stop to the unravelling of his life. Josef described how he invested his entire inheritance with a friend of his, who was supposed to place the money in secure investments. All the money was lost. The friend, in fact, turned out to be a fraudster.

As a result of Josef's carelessness, the relationship with his wife rapidly deteriorated, as she had been looking to the money to smooth out their lives together. Ultimately, she left him. She claimed a sum against Josef so large that the family home was sold; and she took almost all of the money from the sale of their house. Josef still had his job, but his sales numbers were down so far that his job was becoming insecure. He was seeing a therapist and was on anti-anxiety medication.

Josef wanted to ask about a lawsuit against his former friend. Peter was there in the meeting with us to support his brother. Josef added that what made all of this so difficult for him was the fact that the money he had lost was the money his father had worked so long and so hard to accumulate. Josef was evidently in torment as he unburdened himself with his words. Both Peter and I sat in silence while Josef continued with his mournful narrative.

However, Peter broke the silence when Josef said he felt guilty for losing half of their father's money. At that point, Peter said, "I feel guilty, too."

Josef asked, "Why do you feel guilty? Did you also lose father's money?"

"No," said Peter, "I feel guilty because I bought a BMW convertible, and I can't believe that I spent father's hard-earned money on a car that he would never have bought for himself. Now I cannot enjoy the car and I cannot bring myself to spend another dime of father's money. And, I am also feeling guilty because of something I did when I was working at our father's shop during high school. Ever since then, this has been a cloud on my conscience."

Josef looked puzzled, and frankly, I could not understand what Peter was now attempting to confess. Peter continued, "When I was in the shop, I would open the the cash register and take out money when our father went into the cooler. I knew exactly when he would be in there cutting meat. Sometimes, a customer would give me cash and I would wait for the customer to leave and then put it in my back pocket instead of the cash register. Our father was getting blood all over his hands to sell the meat and I was taking the money. With father's money, I was the 'cool' guy to my buddies and the girls, paying for their drinks, and buying their cigarettes. What I was stealing was our family's money."

Peter was losing his composure as he spilled out his anguish over his actions. He buried his face in his hands, then looked at the ceiling, then at Josef, then back at the ceiling. His voice was breaking, "Father,...Josef,...Father,...Josef. I beg you. Please. Forgive me."

Both Josef and I were shocked to hear this confession. Peter turned to Josef, "I love you. I don't want you to get sick over losing our father's money. I will help you with whatever you need. I will never spend our father's money on myself. I owe this to you and to our father."

72. HIS PEN

Jesse was ready to sign his will.

As I handed Jesse one of our office pens, he shook his head, and pulled out his special pen from his jacket pocket. "Do you know how much this pen cost me?" he asked. Without waiting for me to reply, he continued, "$186,000." He then showed it to me up close. It resembled a typical, yet upscale ballpoint pen. When Jesse allowed me to hold it, it did feel heavier than mine did. But $186,000? I could understand perhaps $100 or so, but the price he paid for it seemed astronomical. If not for the sombre look on Jesse's face, I would have felt that this was some sort of preamble to a joke. I asked him if the pen was an antique, or if the pen once belonged to a world-renowned celebrity, or perhaps someone in the Royal Family; but Jesse, for the moment, didn't answer me.

Jesse took back the pen. He initialed every page of the will, inserted the date, signed on the proper line, handed it to me to witness; then I slid the will across the table to the other witness. As she was in the process of initialling the pages, Jesse broke his silence. "I guess you're curious about my pen." I nodded, and he continued. "Franklin, my company's bookkeeper, gave it to me for my 60th birthday. Yes, the day I got this pen, I paid nothing for it. But, two years later, I found out that Franklin had stolen $186,000 from my company. Then he went bankrupt on me. It was at this time that I realized how much this pen really cost me!"

73. THE TALKING DOG

Do you know people who brag about how rich and successful they are, when in fact they are not really who they say they are? And if they really are rich, did they earn their wealth or did they inherit it? If this rings a bell, then the following joke may make you smile.

Jones is driving along a country road and sees a sign next to a farmhouse that reads "talking dog for sale." Having never imagined that a talking dog could exist, Jones immediately stops to inquire if there was any substance to what he read on the sign. He rings the bell at the household to ask about buying the dog.
The farmer, who answers the door, says, "I'm not taking your money until you meet my dog, Wilbur. You can meet him in the barn."

Jones runs to the barn. He looks left and right, and he sees nothing. All of a sudden, from behind a couple of bales of hay comes a voice, "Hiya! How you doin'? How are ya? I'm over here!" Then, Wilbur, the dog, walks out from behind the hay. Jones looks at Wilbur. "Did you just talk to me?" "Sure did," says Wilbur. "I'm a talking dog."

Jones is shocked. "I can't believe a dog can talk!" "That's nothing," says Wilbur. "I make speeches; I write books; and I follow the stock market. I made a fortune for my owner. He made so much money from the stock tips that I gave him, that he bought this farm for cash. I'm famous all over the world. Did you see my speech to the United Nations last year on TV? Did you hear about my inventions? Are you aware that I'm about to win the Nobel Peace Prize?"

Jones is astounded and responds, "I cannot begin to tell you how impressed I am with all of your accomplishments." "Of course," says Wilbur. I'm a self-made dog!"

"I don't care how much you cost. I have to buy you." Wilbur again responds, "Sure enough, I'll make you rich, too! But you'll have to wait until after my meeting with some of the world leaders next week."

Jones runs back to the farmhouse, hoping against hope that no one else has come to see what he has just seen. Jones tells the farmer, "I've got to have that dog! I just have to have that dog! But he must be extremely expensive. What will you take for him?"

The farmer says, "Ahh! Just give me five bucks and you can have him." Jones is shocked. "How come only five dollars for a talking dog who is so accomplished?" The farmer answers, "Because I'm so sick of his bragging. That dog's such a damned liar!"

74. PURE GREED

We had just concluded a call-in television talk show, where we spoke about estate disputes. Our discussion about disputes had captured the interest of Lionel, one of the men who was working in the television studio. Lionel shared his story with us.

His story was about his brother's greed. He and his brother, Phil, were Mom's only children. Mom was a 94-year-old widow, and living in a retirement home that looked after almost all of her needs. However, Lionel commented that even when you are 94, you still expect to enjoy what's left of the rest of your life. Lionel had a lot to say about his brother, Phil's, attitude on this last point.

Mom had moved into the retirement home, taking her 35-year-old bed with her. Lionel wanted to buy her a new bed, as Mom's bed was so old and uncomfortable. Phil objected and refused to allow any of "Mom's money" to be wasted on a new bed. The two brothers spent months arguing about Mom's bed, and only two events led to a compromise over the bed. First of all, the doctor in the residence called to tell them that Mom's back was very sore because she needed better support when she was sleeping at night. Secondly, there was a liquidation sale at one of the furniture outlets, and Phil relented, agreeing to open Mom's purse strings.

Mom liked to carry about two hundred dollars in her purse, which Lionel would withdraw from her account, using her bank card and a bank machine. Mom had appointed Lionel as her attorney under her power of attorney document, because Phil did not want to take on that role. He said his business took up all of his time and that Lionel, who was retired, should deal with Mom's needs.

Lionel would always email Phil on any spending he did for Mom, as the last thing he ever wanted was an accusation that he took any of Mom's money. Even when Lionel withdrew two hundred dollars for Mom, Phil always asked where the money went, and Lionel would tell him it was for Mom's various expenses.

However, as time went on, Phil began to insist that Lionel give him the details as to how the cash withdrawals were being spent. The recollection that came to Lionel's mind was when Mom bought two pairs of pants, each costing $50, had both of them altered for $40, and $60 was the cost of a cut, style, and shampoo for her hair.

When Lionel reported this to Phil, the retort from Phil was, "Why does a 94-year-old woman need to spend so much money on her hair? And why two pairs of pants? Isn't one pair enough for now?"

Mom wanted to go to the symphony, and the tickets were $90. Phil refused, saying that Mom could live without the symphony. "Put on a CD and let her listen to it." So, Lionel paid for the symphony ticket with his own money.

There were many examples of Phil's attempts to shut off any outflow of Mom's funds. Lionel gave two more. As the old TV in her room was beginning to fail, Lionel wanted to get her a new flat-screen TV which had a cost of $300. Phil refused. Lionel bought one with his own money.

When Mom wanted a new dress to attend a family wedding, Phil immediately blocked any discussion, saying that "she should not waste any of her money." Besides, she already had dresses which were good enough to wear, even though they were old. "Have you forgotten that she will soon be 95? How many more weddings do you think Mom will ever attend?" asked Lionel.

Phil raised the temperature of the conflict that was brewing between the two brothers, when he sent Lionel an email containing a large red "STOP" sign which read "STOP SPENDING HER MONEY! It must be preserved for the rest of her life." To this email, Lionel responded by immediately calling Phil, and blasting him on Mom's behalf. "Phil! You sicken me. You're so greedy! You don't really care about preserving any money for Mom; you just want a bigger inheritance for yourself, after she's dead. Hopefully, she'll outlive you!"

Lionel made a good point. Was brother Phil watching Mom's money - or his?

75. I HOPE SHE DIES WITHOUT A WILL

I met Lola at a conference. She was a real estate agent who had formerly been a paralegal. Lola told me that she had lived through a family fight of her own, and felt that there are situations where nothing can ever bring a family back together, once they have been embroiled in an inheritance battle.

Many years ago, her father passed away. After his death, Lola and her mother fought bitterly over his estate. Lola's sister was the only other heir, and she sided with their mother, fighting Lola.

As a result, Lola became estranged from her mother and her sister. Lola despised her mother and her sister, and had not spoken to them for over twenty years. She admitted that there were times when she should have caved in and made up with her mother, even if she had to be an actress and fake it. She knew that her mother could cut her out of her will and totally disinherit her. In fact, Lola had a feeling that her mother had probably already cut her out.

What made matters even more painful for Lola was her recent involvement in a real estate deal which involved a home on the same block as her mother's house. When Lola saw that the value of that home was more than a million dollars, she realized that her mother's house must also be worth that kind of money. That is when Lola expressed her frustration in not having made a false peace with her mother.

Her next comment surprised me when she continued, "I'm sure that if she has a will, I'm not in it; but maybe I'll still get lucky. Maybe she'll lose the will; or, maybe it will get burned up in a fire; or, maybe she hid it and no one will ever find it; and, maybe the old hag will die without a will. I know the law, where there is no will. Since it would only be me and my sister, the law will automatically give me half of my mother's estate. I pray that she doesn't have a will. I could really use that money!"

76. HOW NOT TO MARRY MONEY

Gavin shared a story about what happened to his brother, Max. His story was one of betrayal, greed, and heartbreak. Gavin and Max lived with their father, Alistair, in his luxurious mansion. Alistair was a wealthy real estate developer. He also was a widower in his late eighties.

Gavin's story beings with Max's engagement to Carmelita, who he had met while attending a land development convention in Mexico. Carmelita, who had done some modelling, was one of the hostesses at that convention. Gavin did not go into detail, but had the impression that Carmelita knew that Max came from a very wealthy family.

Max, whose prior experience with women left a lot to be desired, was swept off his feet by Carmelita's attentions to him. Contrary to the usual cold rebuffs which had characterized Max's dealings with women, here was Carmelita, who seemed to be the answer to his prayers. He arranged to fly her home with him to meet his family, and to see where and how the family lived, and, hopefully, to impress her.

When Max arrived at the family mansion with Carmelita, he and Gavin gave her a tour of the homestead, the horse stables, the sports cars, the tennis court, and the private lake. Gavin saw her reaction, and had no doubt that the family wealth had swept Carmelita off her feet. She had to have been impressed, because after being the family guest for only one week, she accepted Max's marriage proposal.

Carmelita's grasp of English was good, and she communicated warmly with the family and their many friends.

It was somewhat delicate for Gavin to express, but he had to say that, as a couple, Max and Carmelita did not look like lovers. As he had already mentioned, she was a model. The same could not be said about his brother. It was hard for Gavin to use the word "homely," but this was a situation that called for honest description, and, yes, Gavin had to say that his brother, Max, was homely. It was, therefore, quite dramatic and uplifting for Max to be about to marry a "trophy wife" like Carmelita.

Homely or not, it was clear that Max appeared to be the focus of Carmelita's attentions. She was constantly flattering him, and telling him how much she loved him.

The wedding day was announced, and invitations were sent out. Gavin's girlfriend, Kathleen, took time off from college and flew in about two weeks before the big day. Carmelita invited four of her friends from Mexico, along with her father, and her mother.

At a pre-wedding party, Carmelita was constantly calling Max, "the love of my life." She even toasted him, addressing him as "my lovely man, my gift from God."

Shortly after that toast, Carmelita went into the kitchen with her parents and friends from Mexico. Laughter and banter filled the air. But the language in the kitchen was Spanish, not English. Gavin's girlfriend, Kathleen, went into the kitchen to join them. She was a stranger to Carmelita, her family and friends, and she wanted to introduce herself. The language immediately shifted to English for these introductions. Carmelita made a point of telling Kathleen that the luckiest day in her life was when she met Max at that land development convention in Mexico. Then, as Kathleen was making her way out of the kitchen, Carmelita's language to her family and friends reverted to Spanish.

Gavin then paraphrased, in English, what Kathleen heard in that kitchen, as Kathleen made her way toward the doorway. "You see," said Gavin, "Kathleen is fluent in Spanish, as she studied Spanish in college, and she is a natural when it comes to languages. Kathleen stopped dead in her tracks as she rounded the corner outside of the kitchen, but fully within earshot of the Spanish dialogue that filled the air. Kathleen never dropped a hint to anyone that she could understand Spanish."

This is roughly what Carmelita exchanged with her parents and her friends, as they saw Kathleen leaving the kitchen:

Mother: "Carmelita, what about Carlos? Aren't you still engaged to him? He is such a handsome man, and he loves you so much. And I know you love him. You make a perfect couple. What happened?"

Carmelita: "He has no money. He's just a plumber. He hardly makes a living."

Friend: "Do you really think Max is that good looking?"

Carmelita: "He's no better looking than a donkey, but I can learn to live with him. It's hard to kiss him but I close my eyes. I don't love him at all."

Father: "If you think he's ugly and you don't love him, why are you getting married to him?"

Carmelita: "Look around you. Everything you see is owned by his father. When the old man dies, and he's got one foot in the grave already, my husband will get half of everything the old man owns. My husband will be rich like a king. When I leave him, I will get a lot of money from my divorce settlement. Then I'll be rich and then I'll be able to marry Carlos, and have a wonderful life with the man I really love."

Kathleen was mortified to hear Carmelita's plot, and told Gavin immediately. Gavin was intent on passing this information on to Max, but before he even had a chance to do it, Kathleen turned to Carmelita, and in Spanish said, "Buenas Noches" (Good Night) and added also in Spanish that she was fluent in the language, understood every syllable that Carmelita spoke, and was horrified that Carmelita would go to those lengths to get someone else's money. When Gavin then told Max what his future wife said, Max was furious. Enraged, Max yelled across the room at Carmelita, "Get the hell out of this house and never come back!"

Gavin ended his story by saying that the only money Carmelita ever got from his family was the money for a one-way plane ticket back to her home in Mexico.

77. HOW MUCH IS A PHONE CALL WORTH?

Minnie had scheduled our appointment well in advance of the date that she met with me. She was here to instruct me to make her new will. She had selected this date specifically so that it fell exactly on the anniversary of her husband's date of death.

She explained that her family situation was very simple. She and her late husband had no children, and, Minnie was an only child. However, her late husband had a dozen nieces and nephews. I looked at the wills that she and her late husband had made. Each of them had left their entire estate to the other. She was inheriting her husband's entire estate. The way her existing will read, her own estate was to be divided equally among her husband's nieces and nephews.

Minnie then spoke of her life with her late husband. They were very frugal people. They had lived together in a rented apartment and drove a very old car. By all outward appearances, they were of very modest means. However, Minnie revealed that, through hard work, disciplined saving, and wise investing, her estate was going to be anything but modest, as her net worth at the time of her appointment exceeded three million dollars.

Then Minnie described her late husband's funeral. Of his dozen nieces and nephews, seven showed up. Minnie had always loved her husband, and the fact that there were five no-shows upset her very much. Of the seven who did show up, only two came up to her to express their condolences. She looked at me, visibly offended, and commented that the other five wouldn't even give her the time of day.

After the funeral, Minnie made a pact with herself, which she now revealed to me. Her estate plan was simple.

Years ago, she promised her husband that if she survived him, she would leave her estate to his nephews and nieces, but she didn't promise him which ones. She would wait one year from the date of her husband's death, to see which of the nieces and nephews would call or visit her. Whoever took the time to call or visit her would inherit; and, if no one called or visited her, she would give everything to charity.

After about four months, Neil, one of her husband's nephews, did call her to ask her how she was doing. He was the only one of the entire group who took the trouble to see if she was alright. In fact, he called her twice, during the year. But, as time revealed, Neil was the only one of the nieces and nephews who seemed to care.

As Minnie was instructing me to give Neil the entire estate under her new will, she said that she would leave a note with her new will telling Neil that he was inheriting her entire estate because he was the only one to take the time and trouble to call her. She then made two comments which struck me.

Her first comment was: "I guess the other eleven had no time to care if I was dead or alive. Because my husband and I lived so frugally, they must have thought that I was too poor to waste their time on."

Minnie's other comment was about Neil, who called her twice: "I'm going to leave a letter with my will. This is what my letter will say. 'Dear Neil. You're the only one who cared about me. You made two phone calls to me, each worth about one-and-a-half-million dollars apiece! I wonder what your cousins will say when you tell them how you struck it rich!'"

The insertion of Minnie's story in this book is not meant to motivate our readers to call their relatives in hopes of hitting it rich like Neil did. However, in our practice as wills and inheritance lawyers, we see that, so many times, decisions about who gets what, and, determining whose name is in or out of the will, are often built upon the simplest of factors - even as seemingly mundane a human action as a phone call.

78. THE CODE

It comes as no surprise that lawyers must be especially sensitive to those who have suffered a personal loss. There are times, though, when the emotions spill over for all involved.

Clyde called our office after his beloved wife, Lorraine, died. Hers was a very unexpected and untimely death, as she left behind Clyde to raise their little six-year-old daughter, Nessa.

When Clyde initially called to make the appointment to discuss Lorraine's will and estate, he asked if I could avoid mentioning Lorraine's name in the presence of Nessa, as he would be bringing her with him to our meeting. He had not yet been able to arrange someone to babysit. He wished to shield Nessa from unnecessary emotions over the loss of her mother. Therefore, we decided between us that all references to Lorraine would be referred to as "the deceased." This was our code word.

The appointment took place in our boardroom, where Nessa took out her book and crayons in order to busy herself. Clyde sat next to her, and I sat opposite to them.

As Clyde and I were discussing the bank accounts, credit card debts, and other assets and liabilities of "the Deceased," little Nessa was quietly crayoning in her book. From time to time, she interrupted Clyde, to show him how she was progressing, and to await her father's praise. Clyde complimented her that she was doing a good job because her crayoning stayed "so well inside the lines."

We began to speak of the house, and, suddenly Clyde slipped when he said that the house was "in Lorraine's name."

The moment he said "Lorraine," Nessa looked up from her book. "Do you know where Mommy is?" she asked. "I want to play hugs and kisses with her."

I was suddenly at a loss for words, and I just looked at Clyde. Before either of us could say anything, Nessa continued, "Mommy just went out to Heaven, and soon she's coming back. Right, Daddy?"

Clyde gently cupped Nessa's chin in his hand and looked into his daughter's eyes. "Sweetheart, you won't see Mommy for a long, long time."

Nessa looked first to me, then back to Clyde; then her innocent gaze rested on me. We were all silent. Another moment passed in frozen silence. Then another. Then another. She was still looking at me, but now she was pleading. "I want to see Mommy NOW!"

Clyde had no idea what to say, nor did I.

True enough, Clyde had slipped up and had been the one to say, "Lorraine" instead of "the deceased." However, I was the one who eventually broke our code with my reaction. What finally released the flow of Nessa's irrepressible torrent of tears was the sight of my tears. Now Nessa knew that her mommy would not be coming back home.

79. MY FAMILY HARDWARE STORE...ITS LEGACY

Imagine a small hardware store established in 1954. Creaky floors, walls covered with every imaginable tool, drawers and bins with every conceivable fastener, screw and nail, people drawn to the store as a place to get advice, trade stories, linger, and tell jokes, and customers being treated as family. The background noises of a paint shaker machine or a key cutter added character to this little store. And when it came to serving customers, "If you want it, Jack will get if for you." Jack somehow had all the answers. Jack seemed to know all of his customers by name; and he always had a smile, a warm handshake, or a pat on the back for whoever came in to shop. Jack was the father of Les, one of the coauthors of this book. Les fondly remembers the days when he operated the store with his late brother, Joel, and his late father, Jack.

"My father, Jack, taught my brother, Joel, and me that the customer should always be treated like a part of our family. Somehow, it didn't occur to me that this worked the other way, too. I never realized how many customers saw my Dad, my brother, and me as part of their family, until after both my father and my brother had passed away. That's when I had to close the store. When I walked by the empty store, former customers would stop me in the street to tell me what that store had meant to them through the years. They said that this was how retail used to be, and how the street would never be the same without Jack's hardware store. Now, 'their store' was closed. But what really motivated me to share my feelings here, about my family's store, came from an email which I received from a former customer. The email reads as follows:

'Dear Les,
You wouldn't remember me, but as a young kid in the 1980's, I would come to your family's store with my mom. I had been away for years, teaching English in South America. I have just returned home, and, today I went to the store with a pack of gum for your dad. (We used to trade gum when I would go in there as a kid.) But I have just learned that Jack, and Joel too, have passed away. And, the store is empty and closed. I wanted to say how truly sorry I am beyond words. They were honestly two very special people. My heart has sunk all day today, and I feel so terrible to hear this news. My sincerest condolences.'

I called to thank him for his touching letter to me. He asked me for my home address. He wanted to send me something in memory of my late father and brother who had meant so much to him.

When I opened the envelope he mailed, there was a letter and a pack of gum. Paraphrasing the letter, it said, 'This is the pack of gum that I was so anxious to give to your dad. I was always excited to go to your store when I was a young boy because I knew that Jack would have gum for me. Now, so many years later, it was my turn to repay him. I had actually bought it as soon as I had come into town, and wanted to surprise him by showing up suddenly at the store. But, I found the store closed. So I wrote to you, Les, and I am sending this gum to you as a tribute to your father and your brother.'

I don't think my dad ever realized how much his kindness and his warmth were loved by his customers. I think about the lessons I learned from him about how to treat other people well. He reminded my brother, Joel, and me so often that everyone should be treated like family. My dad was a very special person and he will always live in my heart."

80. POST SCRIPT: THE IMPORTANCE OF REVIEWING YOUR WILL

A will should not be a "one-size-fits-all" document. It should reflect your own life situation and, therefore, should be reviewed on an ongoing basis.

In our wills practice, we offer the public a free will review. People in our jurisdiction are invited to bring their wills in to our office for this review. As a result, our firm sees a great number of wills. The majority don't have problems, but some wills contain ticking time bombs, which could possibly lead to future family conflict.

Without suggesting that this is an exhaustive list, we would like to share with you, the types of potential problems that have surfaced in what we have seen, so that you might not accidentally create similar errors in your own will.

Remember, when your will comes into effect, you will not be here to explain what you meant, or to help fix the problem.

These are some examples of the potential problems we have seen when people have brought their wills in for us to review them. As a coincidence, there turned out to be 26 of these helpful items - one for each letter of the alphabet. So, you might consider the following as the "abc's" or the "fundamentals" of items to consider when making your will.

a. I saw that his will was done in 1975. The only executor named was his brother, and no alternate executor was named in case the brother died, or if he refused to serve as executor, or if he became incapable to serve as executor. The will was never reviewed until now. I asked how old his brother was. He was 97, and not in good health. The gentleman had simply forgotten that he had named his brother as his only executor. When I asked him if he thought that his brother was the right person to be named as executor, he said that his brother was "definitely not." When I asked if he had thought about naming his children as executors to administer his estate, the gentleman said that he did not realize that a beneficiary could also be named as an executor. He was a widower, and was now going to leave his estate equally to his two children. He was happy to learn that he could name them as executors.

b. I asked the gentleman if he still wanted Doug as alternate executor.
The gentleman's wife has just passed away, and he had appointed her as primary
executor. Now that she was gone, Doug was next in line to be his executor if the
gentleman's will remained unchanged. He was shocked that Doug was still listed
in his will. "I thought I changed it after we broke up our business partnership.
He's still there? I hate him!"

c. I saw that her two grandchildren were named as executors in her will. I asked
her how old they were right now. She said one was 10 and the other was 13.
She was aware that a minor can't serve as an executor, but she felt that it did not
matter because she was adamant that by the time she died, each of her grandkids
would be well over the age of majority. "How do you know that?" I asked.
Her response was, "Trust me, I just know it!"

d. They had named their son-in-law, William, as their primary executor because,
as a banker, he was good with numbers. But when I asked them if they would
still want William to be their executor if he got divorced from their daughter,
they reacted. "We never thought of that. No way!" As a result, they changed their
will to remove William.

e. She had appointed her accountant as her executor. I asked her if her accountant
was agreeable to assume this position when she died. She said that she never
asked him. I immediately told her that she must ask him if he would accept the
role, because, otherwise, she would not know if he would be willing to do it.
An executor named in a will is free to refuse the position. She was surprised to
hear this.

f. She had left everything to her ten nieces and nephews, and appointed all of
them as executors. I asked her if she realized that it would be very likely that she
was introducing deadlock into the administration of her estate because it would
only take one of the ten to either delay a decision or refuse to agree with the
others. I asked her how her ten nieces and nephews got along. I was surprised to
hear her response. Eight of them lived very far away, on another continent, and
she didn't know if any of them knew the others.

g. He left all his "memorabilia" to his son, and the rest of his personal
possessions to his daughter. I told him that the word "memorabilia" lacks

definition, could mean different things to different people, and could require a court interpretation of the word if a dispute breaks out between his children. He responded, "My kids will know what I mean. They'll never fight over that or anything else!" We are used to hearing responses similar to this one from parents but yet, we are also used to hearing about fighting among children over their parents' estates.

h. The clause in her will read, "I leave my diamond ring to my daughter." When I asked her if she had more than one diamond ring, she said she had several. She also described a range of values for the various rings with the lowest value being in the range of $2,000 and the highest being in the vicinity of $20,000. She also mentioned that since the date that she had made her will, she had acquired two more diamond rings. When I asked her how her daughter would know which ring she was supposed to get, the woman had no answer. As a result, she changed her will so that it properly defined exactly which diamond ring her daughter was to get.

i. Her will read, "I leave to my son, any car that I own." When I asked her what kind of a car she owned, she responded, "Last year, I traded my car for a motor home." I told her that her son may be challenged if he tries to take the motor home, as the interpretation of "car" may be too narrow to include a motor home.

j. In her will, she left her piano to her daughter. When I asked her if this is what she still wanted, she seemed surprised and a bit embarrassed, then stated that the will I was reviewing had been made quite a few years ago. In the meantime, she had already given the piano to her son. In fact, it was already in her son's home. She thanked me for reminding her of this. She was now adamant that the clause which left her daughter the piano must be removed from her will, as soon as possible. She wanted to avoid any false expectations her daughter would have, regarding the piano. She said that it would surely be easier and better on the family for her to now remove the clause in her will, than for her son to possibly have to move the piano from his house.

k. Her will attempted to regulate the manner in which her three children would deal with her personal effects after she passed away. But I pointed out to her that allowing her eldest child to have the first pick, the next eldest to have the second pick, and her youngest child, the third pick, was possibly unfair.

When she asked how that could be unfair, I gave the following example: The most expensive item by far may be a valuable painting, and the eldest may choose that. The next most expensive item may have a value many thousands of dollars below the first item chosen by her eldest. This never crossed her mind. She then realized that a neutral method, such as picking their names from a hat, for the first and second choices, may be a better method and avoid squabbling among her children.

l. His will was ten years old. It left a number of gifts to various people. When I asked him if there were any major changes to his life since he had made his will, he replied, "Yes, last year I got married." I had the unpleasant duty to tell him that in our jurisdiction, subject to some technical exceptions, marriage revokes a will which was made before the date of the marriage. I had to let him know that his will was null and void.

m. His will contained very elaborate instructions relating to his funeral, his burial, and the disposition of his remains. It appeared evident that these instructions, which included an expensive and elaborate after-death party, would seriously erode his estate assets, and might even exhaust all of the assets in his estate. I had to tell him that, in our jurisdiction, these decisions were to be made by his executor, and, if the instructions in his will led to extraordinary and unreasonable expense, his executor could choose to arrange a more modest funeral and burial.

n. He left $5,000 to "each of my buddies at work." I asked him who they were. He replied that they knew who they were. My response was that this wording was too vague, because anyone who was an employee of his company could claim to have been one of his "buddies." To avoid a serious estate problem, he decided to name each of the "buddies" by name in his new will.

o. Her nephew was her only living relative. He was a drug addict. In order to protect her nephew from squandering the estate, her homemade will set up a trust consisting of everything she would own when she died. This trust would be managed for her nephew for the rest of his life. The problem, however, was that her will did not mention what would happen to what was left in this trust after her nephew died. The glaring omission was the failure to name a person or a charity to receive the balance of the trust money after her nephew passed away.

p. Her will said that her son would only get his inheritance if "after I die he divorces his witch wife from Trinidad." I had to tell her that the clause would probably be successfully challenged in court as being against principles of public policy.

q. His will said, "I have loaned money to my daughter, and the money she owes me shall be deducted from her share of my estate." When I asked him what she owed him now, he said that his daughter had paid it all back to him years ago. Therefore, I suggested that he amend his will to remove that clause. Otherwise, he would be creating a false impression among his other children, which may cause them to claim that his daughter reduce her share. She would be put in a position of having to produce evidence that she paid this debt, years after any records of repayment may have disappeared. Worst of all, the one person who could clear up the problem, being the man in front of me, would no longer be alive to say that she had paid back every nickel.

r. When I examined his will, I saw that his entire estate was left to his only child, his daughter, and if she predeceased him, her children would inherit in her place. He said that he did not like his son-in-law, and didn't want his son-in-law to get a "red cent" of his estate. I suggested to him that if his daughter inherited his estate, and was later involved in a marriage breakdown, there was a real possibility that his son-in-law would be able to benefit from money made from her inheritance. He asked me if there was a way to avoid this. I said that in our jurisdiction, there is a clause, often referred to as the "family law clause," which protects the income made by a married child's inheritance in the event of separation or divorce. However, that clause was missing from his will. He was determined to make an amendment to his will to include that clause.

s. His will read, "I leave my entire estate to my children equally." When I asked him how many children he had, he said he had four adult children who were living here, each of whom he loved dearly. Then he mentioned that he had another adult child in another country as a result of a short-term relationship. He had not seen or heard from that child in over thirty years. I told him that the wording of his will would also include that estranged child. I explained that the estranged child would be able to inherit because that child was a member of the class he set up. The words "my children" that he put in his will set up a class gift, which would include all of his children regardless of how he felt about them. He decided to make a brand-new will, specifically naming the four children that he really wished to inherit from him.

t. Her will left everything equally to her two children. This sounded straightforward enough until she went on to mention that one of her children was now disabled and was receiving government benefits under a government disability support program. I told her that under the legislation in our jurisdiction, that son would lose his government benefits as soon as she died because the inheritance would be large enough to disqualify her son from receiving any benefit under that program. She was alarmed when I explained this and asked if there was a way to allow her son to keep getting his benefits. I told her that there was a type of trust she could establish in her will which would not disqualify her son from receiving these benefits. This type of trust would give her executors absolute discretion over the money for the disabled beneficiary. It is referred to as a type of "absolute discretionary trust." She immediately wanted to have that type of trust in her new will.

u. Her 35-year-old will had been done shortly after her husband had passed away. It gave everything to her three children. To this point, her will did reflect her wishes. However, due to the fact that she had no grandchildren at the time the will was signed, she had now created a potential problem. Her will went on to provide that if any one or two of the three children passed away before she did, then her estate would be divided by the other or others. In other words, if one child died before her, the estate would go to the other two children; and if two died before her, the remaining child would inherit the entire estate. Her problem now came from the fact that she wanted to avoid a grandchild being cut out of her will if the parent of that grandchild predeceased her. She asked for a solution, which meant that her new will would have to provide that if any of her children who had a child or children (in other words, a grandchild) predeceased her, the share of such predeceased child would go to that grandchild.

v. His signed and witnessed will consisted of four lines. It named an executor, back-up executor, a beneficiary, and back-up beneficiary. When he asked if that was good enough, I told him that the will was lacking many of the powers that his executor would need. It is, as a rule, good policy to give generous powers to your executor so that he or she can do, after your death, all that you could do in life, so that your estate can be administered in an efficient manner. Among other powers, some of the powers which should be inserted in a will are: (a) the power to sell and convert assets to cash, (b) the power to retain assets in their existing form, (c) the power to pay debts, and, (d) the power to deal with real estate.

w. The first sentence in his will read, "This is my last will and power of attorney." I explained to him that a power of attorney and a will are very different documents. A power of attorney is effective only while you are living. It terminates on your death. On the other hand, a will is not effective until you die. It has no effect during your lifetime; and, the executor named in your will has no power to act during your lifetime. In our jurisdiction, as in many others, you need three key estate planning documents: (a) a power of attorney for personal care where you appoint someone you trust to deal with your health and personal care issues; (b) a financial power of attorney where you appoint someone you trust to deal with your assets while you are alive; and, (c) a will which dictates what you want done to finalize your estate after you are gone.

x. He was in his second marriage. He came in alone for me to review his will, which left all of his personal effects including furniture, books, plates, and silverware to the children of his first marriage. I asked him how his second wife would react if his children went into his apartment after his death and started taking paintings off the walls, furniture from the dining room, and china from the cabinet. What if his second wife stated that she either bought these items or got them as a gift from her family? Did he ever discuss this with his second wife? Were there any lists which were agreed upon and which showed the ownership of what was on those lists? Could his children show receipts or evidence that a certain item belonged to him and not to his second wife? After hearing these questions from me, he realized that he was on the path to creating a potential battle between his second wife and the children of his first marriage.

y. Her circumstances had changed since she had made her will, and she asked me if it needed updating, or was the way it was written, adequate. It left everything to her daughter, and, if her daughter did not survive her, then it left everything to her only grandchild. Her daughter was her only executor, and there was no back-up executor named. Then she told me that her daughter was killed in a car accident last year. I told her that based upon what her will said, her granddaughter, who was currently 13 years of age, would inherit; but the full inheritance would come to her at 18.

She said that when she had made her will, she never dreamt that her daughter would die before her. I told her that firstly, there should be a backup beneficiary to inherit in the event that her granddaughter died before her. She also mentioned that her assets were substantial: over five million dollars currently, and still growing. I asked her if she felt it was reasonable and practical to leave this kind of an estate to an 18-year-old. The lady agreed that there was a high risk of her estate being squandered. She, therefore, felt that an 18-year-old should not be able to access this kind of an estate. She agreed with my suggestions that there should be a new executor named, with a back-up executor, to manage and administer a trust for her granddaughter until she was mature enough to get her hands on this large estate.

Deciding upon the right age is a personal matter; but, people who make a trust of this nature usually consider 25 to 30 as the appropriate age range. The lady agreed that as it was currently written, her will was certainly not adequate.

z. He brought in a lawyer-prepared will that left eleven people various gifts of money. On five of the gifts, the names of the beneficiaries were scratched out with a pen, and new names and amounts were written in on the line above where the original names were typed. Although the will itself was signed by the gentleman and two witnesses, the only initials beside the scratched out beneficiary lines belonged to the gentleman. There were no initials of witnesses beside the changes he made. He asked me if this was going to be acceptable when he died. I told him that in order to make the changes he wanted, certain legal formalities were required; and, if they were not followed, such changes would not be recognized by the law.

A codicil is the recommended method of making such changes. It is normally used for minor amendments to an existing will. It is a separate document from the will, and it supplements, subtracts, or makes additions to an existing will. A person is allowed to have more than one codicil, but it is not recommended to exceed two, so as not to complicate the interpretation of the will. Each codicil multiplies the effort involved in interpreting the original will. It is advisable, wherever possible, that a person should create a new will, as opposed to imposing multiple codicils upon an executor.

APPENDICES

THE FOLLOWING LYRIC WAS WRITTEN BY LES KOTZER TO PAY TRIBUTE TO HIS LATE PARENTS, ROSE AND JACK KOTZER.

YOU MADE THE DIFFERENCE

I could have walked a different path
Or traveled down a winding road
Of all the debts I've ever owed, my greatest is to you
You made a difference
You made a difference
You made the difference in my life

I might have taken foolish risks
Or overlooked the danger signs
You were there behind me all the time
You made a difference
You made a difference
You made the difference in my life

CHORUS
    It would be naive to say
    That I'd get there anyway
    How do I repay you?

    What is left for me to say?
    To thank you for the gentle way
    You made the difference to my life

I might have struggled to find myself
Or searched for love along the way
In a world that sometimes makes no sense, you gave me confidence
You made a difference
You made a difference
You made the difference in my life

    Your love is the greatest gift I've ever known and
    You made the difference in my life

You made a difference
You made a difference
You made the difference in my life

You made the difference in my life

With the permission of Lewis Manne, Wendy Watson and Les Kotzer
To hear this song visit www.touchyourheartsongs.com

THE WILLS LAWYERS: THEIR STORIES OF:
Money, inheritance, greed, family and... BETRAYAL

THE FOLLOWING LYRIC WAS WRITTEN BY LES KOTZER
TO PAY TRIBUTE TO THE SPECIAL BOND BETWEEN HIM
AND HIS LATE BROTHER, JOEL KOTZER

CANDLES ON THE CAKE

Little boy
running home
school day in December

He was there
with open arms
The things that we remember

Songs we heard
Special words
at birthday celebrations

Wishes made
Games we played
with childish expectations

Sentimental moments
are all that we can take
Childhood disappears
just like the candles on the cake

Little boy
years ago
with family and his friends

Closed his eyes
and made a wish
that it would never end

Blowing out the candles
that December afternoon
Life was picture perfect
How did it end so soon?

And now that time has passed
There are nights I lie awake
So vivid in my thoughts
He lights the candles on the cake

Sentimental moments
are all that we can take
Childhood fades away
Just like the candles on the cake

BARRY M. FISH AND LES KOTZER
HAVE ALSO CO-AUTHORED 3 OTHER BOOKS:

- The Family Fight… Planning to Avoid it

- The Family War… Winning the Inheritance Battle

- Where There's an Inheritance… Stories from Inside the World of Two Wills Lawyers

If you wish to order any of these publications,
please visit www.familyfight.com or call 1 (877) 439-3999.

Les Kotzer is also a professional songwriter. Listen to samples of his songs at
www.touchyourheartsongs.com. He can be reached by email at les@leskotzer.com